Praise for *Courage to Execute*

"I've worked with Jim; he knows his stuff, and this book is proof of that. *Courage to Execute* is full of proven tactics and techniques to drive business success by applying military principles, some of which we've deployed at The Home Depot. What I admire most about Jim's work is that he understands that at the heart of every strategy ... at the core of every successful campaign ... are people."

— Carol Tomé,
Chief Financial Officer and Executive Vice President,
Corporate Services, The Home Depot

"In *Courage to Execute*, ex-fighter pilot Jim Murphy explains the proven frameworks and techniques used by our military's highest performing units to drive Flawless Execution while performing at the highest levels. He clearly and simply adapts those tools for business leaders who want to improve their teams' execution at any level. It is a great read full of practical insights and tools to drive executional excellence."

— Mike White,
Chairman and CEO, DirecTV

"Jim Murphy's work with us and his latest book *Courage to Execute* have truly disrupted—in a positive way—how our business thinks and executes. The motion picture industry doesn't just need to make films about the military, we need to adopt their tactics! Businesses across the spectrum can learn from this book and Murphy's experience, which can accelerate anyone's performance."

— Ryan Kavanaugh
CEO, Relativity Media, LLC

"As an Army Aviator and current business executive, I am convinced that the principles and tactics of our military's high-performing teams hold valuable lessons for American business. *Courage to Execute* brings those lessons home. Simplicity *does* combat complexity!"

— Colonel Lawrence M. Iwanski, U.S. Army Reserve,
Executive Director, Financial Services
at a leading financial services provider

"You can't travel far in corporate America without hearing about Jim Murphy and the radical things he and his company are doing. Murphy is the hands down voice of successful companies and elite corporate warriors everywhere. *Courage to Execute* is his third, and by far his best book yet. Navy SEALs. Army Rangers. And all the tools the rest of us need to be SEALs in our own lives. Highly recommended."

— L. Douglas Keeney,
Former Vice President, Young & Rubicam,
and Author of *15 Minutes* (St.Martin's Press/Macmillan)

"In *Courage to Execute*, Jim 'Murph' Murphy artfully blends the lessons learned during an inspirational military career into practical, applicable guidance that effectively translate to the civilian business world. Jim provides historical content that validates the advice and direction provided. He weaves first hand wins from business and professional sports to further advance the realization of what can be accomplished in our efforts to achieve our specific High Definition Destinations (HDD), while leveraging simplicity over complexity.

"Murphy incorporates components of his book, *Flawless Execution*, with new, powerful insight that aids the reader in victoriously attacking his/her real world, real pressure, high risk, high reward environment.

"As a child of both the military and corporate America (IBM Corporation) I have lived the framework so well-articulated in *Courage to Execute* and been the benefactor of its processes and systems. This is a wonderful tutorial to success as seen through the eyes of an American military hero and entrepreneur.

— Steven W. Tomson,
Director of Sales, ProfitStars
Jack Henry & Associates, Inc.

COURAGE
TO
EXECUTE

What Elite U.S. Military Units Can Teach Business about Leadership and Team Performance

JAMES D. MURPHY

WILEY

For general information about our other products and services, please contact our Customer Care Department within the United States at (800) 762-2974, outside the United States at (317) 572-3993 or fax (317) 572-4002.

Wiley publishes in a variety of print and electronic formats and by print-on-demand. Some material included with standard print versions of this book may not be included in e-books or in print-on-demand. If this book refers to media such as a CD or DVD that is not included in the version you purchased, you may download this material at http://booksupport.wiley.com. For more information about Wiley products, visit www.wiley.com.

Library of Congress Cataloging-in-Publication Data:

Murphy, James D., 1954–
   Courage to execute : What elite U.S. military units can teach business about leadership and team performance / James D. Murphy.
      pages cm
   Includes bibliographical references.
   ISBN 978-1-118-79009-0 (cloth); ISBN 978-1-118-84130-3 (ebk); ISBN 978-1-118-84132-7 (ebk)
   1. Management. 2. Leadership. 3. Success in business. I. Title.
   HD31.M823 2014
   658.4'01–dc23

                                                                                          2013035594

Printed in the United States of America

10 9 8 7 6 5 4 3 2 1

CONTENTS

PREFACE

Elite military warriors are trained to perform at exceptionally high levels. They're put through the paces until they have the individual skills necessary to accomplish their missions, then these warriors come together as a team. They come from all walks of life but emerge from their training as Army Rangers or Navy SEALs. It doesn't take a pedigree and it isn't a birthright. You have to earn it. If you want to make the cut and be on that team, you need determination, motivation, confidence, courage, and the willingness to sacrifice your personal identity for the group's identity.

None of that is easy—the washout rate is high—but there are some encouraging words here. The first is training. In truth, you don't need special skills or background to become the best of the best—our entire military establishment was designed to take a diverse group of young people straight off the streets and put them into a process that molds them into fighter pilots, Rangers, SEALs, and ultimately enables them to execute in the business world outside the military. One day I was a farm boy from Kentucky, then entered the process. Next thing I knew, I was an F-15 fighter pilot. A decade later, I was teaching companies how to execute like a well-trained squadron. True story. And all because of a process.

You see, people who become elite in any field go against the grain and challenge accepted theories. Sometimes, conventional wisdom holds that the elite are somehow born, not made, that they came to their status naturally, not through training. That's simply not true. As the pages ahead will show you, you *can* train perfection, you *can* train courage, and guess what? You can train to become elite. It's not about luck or the right school or good genes. It's about you.

I'd barely learned to fly a Cessna when the air force took me off the streets and started making me into a top-notch fighter pilot. Not long after, I was flying a supersonic fighter jet over that farm in Kentucky. I wanted it. I worked hard. I made the cut. But I had no special skills. Need more proof? Just look around. There are plenty of examples of individuals and teams becoming extraordinary. It just takes a process.

You'd think everyone knows that. But in my years working with some of the most successful organizations in the world, I've found that most leaders have trouble actualizing that knowledge—implementing and following the processes they know can take them to the next level. It really hit me in the fall of 2011. If anyone was executing well, I thought surely it was the NFL. Then as we began working with teams like the Packers, Giants, and Broncos, we learned that everyone struggles to find and follow a winning process. The New York Giants' season had started slowly, they were having trouble. Then they began adopting elements of our military-inspired model and things began to change. They began winning and by Christmas, they were Super Bowl contenders. They continued improving and in February, they won the 2012 Super Bowl, crediting hard work, each other, and our process.

Organizations like the Broncos and Giants felt alone in the struggle to execute; they thought everyone else was doing it better. What we've discovered is that most businesses and teams have not learned what I learned in the military. Individual execution is one thing, but organizational execution is everything. And it shouldn't be as complex as the world we're competing in.

Inspired by the Giants, we went back and looked at our country's elite warriors and their history. We examined the spec ops community, aircraft carrier operations, aerial performance teams, and more. We began to see the patterns, the traits that give teams what I call the courage to execute. We found that every member of every elite team came in without any particular gifts—but they had all been trained, they had been indoctrinated with common standards and values, they had all rehearsed the scenarios they would face. What seems confusing and bewildering to you or me looks like a walk in the park to them. They're so well trained that they view a demanding mission as just "executing the plan." They know to keep it simple, and just follow the process.

In the pages that follow, you'll see how our elite military forces execute, and through these examples you'll learn how to develop, hone, and spread their ability to execute across your entire organization. You just need determination to be the best. One day I was a farm boy, the next, an F-15 fighter pilot. Process. Now you can see how that process works for some of our nation's finest, in the most challenging of conditions. And you'll see some spectacular results.

ACKNOWLEDGMENTS

I'd like to thank the many men and women who, over the past 18 years, have had an effect on this book. Countless fighter pilots and special operations professionals have come through our doors at Afterburner and have all contributed to this work and the Flawless Execution model.

We have also learned so much from our clients as they have leveraged and deployed these techniques in every type of business in every corner of the globe. Flawless Execution is a never-ending journey to find the best way to improve efficiently on the battlefield, in the marketplace, or in life. It's a collective work of lessons from practitioners who are not academic but pragmatic in using techniques that drive results. Our practitioners hail from elite military teams, surgical teams, and teams operating in high-risk environments, as well as the most successful of capital enterprises, all the way to the NFL.

A special thank-you to my writing partners, Alvin Townley and Will Duke, who have taken our model and captured its true essence of *using simplicity to combat complexity*.

And I would like to dedicate this book to the brave men and women serving in our military as well as my loving father, who has taught me so much about family, pursuit, and happiness.

— Murph

CHAPTER 1

THE MILITARY RESPONSE TO A COMPLEX WORLD: THE NEW VALUE OF EFFECTIVE EXECUTION

It was Thursday, March 20, 2003, the first night of the Iraq War.

No moon. Calm seas. Perfect night for a surprise raid by an elite special operations force.

Four Mark V SOCs (Special Operations Craft) were running flat out across the Persian Gulf. Two boats were loaded with Navy SEALs. Their pockets were filled with ammunition; their faces were blackened. They were dead serious. Just hours before they'd launched, their boat team leader—a 26-year-old Harvard graduate—had told them, "We're going to change the world tonight. Let's do it right." Then his team embarked on one of the first missions in this new war. His men were ready for their task, ready to show the courage to execute.[1]

From the boats, they looked out toward their rapidly-closing target: the Mina al-Bakr Oil Terminal, an impressive complex jutting out in the Gulf. The facility handled virtually all of Iraq's crude oil exports and American intelligence assets were convinced that Iraqi forces planned to unleash environmental and financial havoc by blowing up the facility; the SEALs were there to make sure that it didn't happen.

The seconds ticked off the clock, and each second mattered. The raid was supposed to have occurred at the very outset of hostilities, but the air war had started early, so the SEALs knew the Iraqis at the terminal would be on high alert, and more prepared by the minute. Every SEAL had a different scenario running through his mind as he tried to suppress the nervousness that naturally surfaces before combat. No matter how much training they'd had, these professionals all knew things could go terribly wrong in battle. *Stay calm. Stay focused.* Had they missed anything? Perhaps. No team can ever enter a battle with perfect knowledge. You gather your best intelligence, you plan, you brief, and you go. Then you adapt along the way. That's part of the process.

They watched as their brightly lit target approached, and they steadied themselves as the thumping of the boats rattled their teeth. To a

---

[1]James Dao, "A Nation at War: The Commandos; Navy Seals Easily Seize 2 Oil Sites," *New York Times*, March 22, 2003. www.nytimes.com/2003/03/22/world/a-nation-at-war-the-commandos-navy-seals-easily-seize-2-oil-sites.html.

man they were ready, each loaded with weapons, armor, and ammo. They knew the plan; they'd rehearsed it. They'd briefed it again that night. They believed in it. They were ready and this was their mission. This was the opening round of the Iraq War, and their job was to secure the terminal. Simple, direct, achievable.

One SEAL looked at his watch and nodded to the others. The boats slowed and quietly motored out from the dark of night into the halo of light surrounding the oil terminal. The SEALs pulled up beside a ladder. Silently, the men exited the boats and began climbing stealthily toward the upper decks. The team fanned out in perfect order and found their first hostile. He surrendered. Several SEALs bound him while others moved on. Whispered words spoke quietly but crisply from their headsets as the assault team approached the room where they expected the rest of the soldiers would be. With emotionless precision, they swiftly took down the door, swept in, and found 20 Iraqi soldiers turning in complete surprise. The SEALs' shouts mixed with the Iraqi soldiers' cries; hands went up quickly and the room surrendered to the American special forces team.

Phase one was good, phase two was a go. An interpreter began interrogating the Iraqi leaders, the SEALs learned that the Iraqi government had paid them to destroy the terminal, along with themselves and any interfering U.S. forces. As the team members continued their mission, they found explosive charges placed at strategic points throughout the facility. Had the charges been detonated, the facility would have been destroyed and untold amounts of crude oil would have poured into the Persian Gulf.

Within minutes, the SEALs had secured the entire platform, which contained more than three miles of decking and even more piping. They had achieved their goal with no loss of life or property. The mission had gone exactly according to plan. In some ways, they were lucky. But luck usually comes from good preparation. Later, when reflecting on the raid, one of the team leaders considered how this night had been tough—they'd effectively opened the war—but in fact had been nothing more than the expected result of a long deliberate process of SEAL training: fitness and indoctrination, core skills and specialties, teamwork, planning, execution, debriefing, and leadership, all first learned in the infamous Basic Underwater Demolition/SEAL training program widely known as BUD/S. Aspiring SEALs enter a carefully-designed process—essentially the same methodical military regimen that produces elite teams of warriors for the army, air force, and marines. When our newly trained special forces operators graduate, regardless of their branch, they're prepared to execute flawlessly on any battlefield, the world over.

That night on the Persian Gulf was one more element of proof.

So, how do members of America's elite military units execute at such high levels? Do they have natural abilities and instincts that the rest of us don't have? Are they by nature the bravest of men? Were they predestined from birth to be supremely fit men of action who can work together to achieve almost any goal under nearly any circumstance? Not at all.

Yes, they are brave. They confront and overcome all manner of challenges in pursuit of their goals. But they weren't born with these abilities, nor did they necessarily have them when they first volunteered to serve. Their courage, confidence, and capabilities stem from a relentless, time-proven process of conditioning, training, planning, executing, and improving. They are brave and capable because they have been prepared to be brave and capable. They enter battle in top physical condition (resulting from months or years of regimented training), they know the plan (which they've helped to develop), and they've committed all the details to memory. They trust each other; they've considered every contingency. They understand their goal and the consequences of failure. They're bought in, aligned, and they have the confidence to execute the most challenging missions.

Training is of course key. Spec ops team leaders have organized their men according to their abilities; they've clearly defined the role of each man. They don't operate as a rank-based hierarchy, but as a group of professionals, each accountable for specific tasks. From that accountability arises trust. In the field, these operators share information as they receive it and incorporate it into their battle plan, which remains flexible even as their goal remains constant. The team may encounter surprises, but that won't alter their process—in fact, that's *part* of their process. They expect surprise and when it occurs, they simply adapt, adjust, and continue pursuing their mission.

Perhaps above all, these men are more disciplined than almost any other team on the planet. They are wholly focused on their mission and they will execute every action patiently and with unshakable confidence. They do this not because they're arrogant or naïve, not because they think they're invincible or superior to their foe, but because they have prepared, they have honed their process, and they trust one another implicitly. Courage is not bravado; it's forged through a regimented process. And that process is uninterested in your pedigree and blind to politics. That process takes raw soldiers and manufactures elite warriors. Twelve months after its raid on the oil terminal, that finely-tuned team of SEALs would look very different. Veterans would leave, replaced by new members who brought their own experience. But that team, and every spec ops team, would continue to function at its previous high level. The military's common process and the SEALs' core principles remain a constant and ensure consistency, even during periods of turnover. The new simply replaces the old, according to the process that makes these warriors.

American business could use some of our military's elite men and women, and the process they use to execute their missions. You see, American business has a problem. It's not a strategy problem or an analysis problem. And it's not a measurement problem or a capital problem or an education problem; we have plenty of gifted people, innovative ideas, and financial resources. We have an abundance of great plans developed by specialized in-house task forces or highly-paid external consultants. Our corporations have wise boards, make great products, and are smart operators—yet they consistently fail to meet goals and can't figure out why. Organizations will spend valuable resources to deliver new training or to develop new methodologies that only make a complex business more complicated. The end result of all this activity? Businesses still don't get the results they want.

Why? American business has an *execution* problem. Complexity is the mortal enemy of good execution, and our world is nothing if not increasingly complex. Good execution demands simplicity, and in the military, we combat complexity with simplicity. We take a team of SEALs, give them a mission, and send them on their way. Secure the platform; use your training. Simplicity.

When the global war on terror began in 2001 with Operation Enduring Freedom, few real fronts existed, even in Afghanistan. On the ground in the Hindu Kush mountains, and virtually around the world, the U.S. military found itself fighting terrorists in caves and on the Internet. Modern warfare is marked by complex networks that resist change and have less and less central control, yet they evolve faster than ever. Fronts appear, disappear, and reappear. Friends and foes are hard to distinguish. Welcome to the asymmetrical battlespace.

The business world is just as complex and market competition changes just like those modern battlefields. Today, a savvy entrepreneur with a pocketful of capital can fundamentally alter a marketplace once dominated by Fortune 500 stalwarts. New apps and business models render old ones obsolete—then new companies get outinnovated and replaced themselves. Sometimes, innovative firms can make legacy companies more profitable, if the legacy companies are forward-thinking enough to act. Companies like Priceline and Uber helped the travel and transportation industries by allowing traditional companies to sell excess capacity to consumers at a discount. Smart organizations are always looking to exploit new opportunities, adapt their business model to keep pace with the rate of change, and stay alive.

Many organizations have combated this complexity with even more complexity. Countless books, articles, and theorists offer myriad models to analyze markets, formulate strategy, develop products, enhance execution, and measure sales teams. What do they have in common? They're just as complicated as the world they're trying to simplify.

Increasing the level of complexity to solve a problem doesn't work. It never has.

When World War II Allied supreme commander Dwight Eisenhower left the White House after serving eight years as president, he warned the public about the military-industrial complex, that group of industries closely tied to national defense. Today, there is another rising complex and it poses a serious threat to the very people it claims to help. We call these groups the *business-intellectual complex*. Between books, magazines, seminars, and schools, it's a staggeringly-large, multibillion-dollar industry. Articles, experts, and dissertations abound that interpret trends, teach strategic planning, offer sales advice, or provide new management models. Thousands of students attend one of hundreds of U.S. business schools each year.

Here's the thing: The U.S. military gets extremely high levels of execution from teams with members who are often under age 21, most with no college education. These teams perform at extremely high levels in the most demanding, high-stakes environments imaginable—and on G.I. pay. Their secret?

A simple, replicable process to make them elite warriors.

Thankfully, those processes easily transfer to business and you can just look at Todd Ehrilch to see them at work.

At the beginning of the twentieth century, the beverage industry's soft-drink battlefront ran between Coca-Cola and Pepsi. It was a simple environment, Coke versus Pepsi with a few stragglers on the edges. Now it's the Wild West. Dr. Pepper, Snapple, Red Bull, Arden's Garden, and countless others products, including a recovery drink called Kill Cliff.

After leaving the Navy, former SEAL operator Todd Ehrlich became an entrepreneur. During his military service, he learned that inflammation contributed to numerous health problems. He saw a void in the beverage market and decided to develop a sports drink that would help fight internal inflammation. He came up with Kill Cliff recovery drinks, which restock a body's lost electrolytes and fight swelling.

Ehrlich sold his first case of Kill Cliff in 2012 and ever since, he's waged a challenging but successful campaign to grow sales and spread the benefits of his product. But it wasn't easy. Competitive forces fought back; retailers were skeptical. Kill Cliff often had to take bad terms or delayed payment to get shelf space; occasionally, they had to promise to buy back any unsold product. To succeed, Ehrlich and his sales team had to take their lumps until they could prove that their products could deliver.

"As a Navy SEAL, I wouldn't have ever picked a fight with the Chinese army," explained Ehrlich. "So as a start-up beverage company competing against established giants, I have to use small unit tactics, just like the SEALs. We don't play their game; I'll beat them in other ways."

First, like special operations forces going into a new territory, Kill Cliff's employees set out to win hearts and minds. They began low-budget campaigns to sponsor trainers at local gyms. When members saw trainers wearing Kill Cliff T-shirts, they inevitably asked about the product. Kill Cliff couldn't compete with sponsors in established sports leagues like the NBA or NFL, but they could make headway at the Ultimate Fighting Championship. One November night three Kill Cliff–sponsored fighters fought and each won. The trio of victories helped spread the word and build the brand.

Second, Kill Cliff hammers and pivots with extraordinary agility. It can attack competitors head-on, or call in a strike on their flanks. It can quickly change strategies or marketing thrusts. The company's employees can also pivot. In SEAL platoons, at least two men can do any given job. "One is none, and two is one," goes the spec ops saying, and Cliff Kill is no different. The company hired employees with unique as well as overlapping skills so they can approach problems from different perspectives. Experts on one subject can also handle secondary roles when manpower runs thin.

Third, Kill Cliff built a sense of identity around the company and created a sense of mission among its people. At first they found young men and women who were willing to work for free, who believed in the product and the team's philosophy. Ehrlich himself took no pay for nearly two years and his first salesman had no salary for nine months. The shared sacrifice created a cohesive team that built camaraderie and trust.

Fourth, the team was prepared for contingencies. "We have to be prepared," Ehrlich said. "Because it usually takes longer than you plan and something always comes up. You have to be prepared financially and mentally."

In a word, Ehrlich transformed his start-up into an elite team of warriors and applied his SEAL training to his desired outcome—to establish his brand as a serious competitor in the sports drink market.

"As a SEAL or start-up, you have to have the tenacity to see the mission through on the bad days when the wind is in your face," Ehrlich said. "Sometimes during BUD/S your goal might have been just to finish one set of pushups. But you set goals and reach them; we do the same thing at Kill Cliff. We set daily goals that keep us moving forward, focused on what's most important. And we get there." Kill Cliff responded to asymmetry just like its founder had learned during basic training: by developing new tactics, combating complexity with simplicity, and never quitting. In SEAL parlance, he never *rang the bell*, the signal a SEAL candidate is dropping out.

Should Coke, Pepsi, and other giants worry about a small competitor like Kill Cliff?

Absolutely. There is an array of specialty providers like Kill Cliff, slowly chipping away at established market leaders. With fewer barriers to entry, revenues will go to the nimble and quick-to-adapt. If larger companies can't or don't adapt, they'll suffer.

Those larger companies haven't taken this lying down. Coca-Cola has diversified by acquiring brands like Vitamin Water and Monster energy drinks. They've improved niche appeal with brands like Odwalla and Gold Peak Tea. Likewise, legacy brewer Anheuser Busch responded to the surging popularity of microbrews with Shock Top and Goose Island. Many consumers have no idea that microbrew lookalike Shock Top and Chicago-brewed Goose Island are owned by Anheuser Busch—and that's just fine with Anheuser Busch, who is busy building these niche brands. Forward-thinking large firms are learning how to handle changing market trends and push an entrepreneurial mind-set through their organization. They're learning to grow corporate value while benefitting from the niche appeal and nimbleness of subbrands and subsidiaries. Many are driving authority to lower levels of the organization. But they still face tough competition from smart and savvy upstarts.

Whether you're leading a raid on an oil terminal, running a start-up, or leading a corporate division, you can learn from the clear and simple military process that created leaders like Todd Ehrlich, along with high-performing teams, just like the one that secured Mina al-Bakr. To implement its process, the military indoctrinates its recruits and new officers with the basic values and skills they need to succeed as individuals and teams. Then, these individuals become specialists and learn to align their role on a team with any given mission. They're taught to plan deliberately and brief the plan before executing it. With each soldier or sailor depending on another in combat, they learn responsibility. In postoperation debriefs they hold each other accountable while distilling lessons learned that they'll use in the next mission. The military trains us to be accountable, to simplify, to align and empower others, and to know the process that builds men and women into elite performers. As our servicemen and women repeat this cycle again and again, they can become extraordinary leaders who have the training, experience, and confidence to act. They have the *courage to execute*. American business can develop the same thing.

MISSION BRIEF

In the chapters ahead, you'll see that:

1. In a complex world, simplicity combats complexity.
2. A clear, simple process will improve an organization's ability to execute and achieve its goals.
3. Effective plans come from a deliberate six-stage planning process that begins with the end in mind.
4. Specific mission objectives should be clear, measurable, and achievable, and aligned with a high-definition destination.
5. Briefing the plan is critical to good execution.
6. Task saturation presents the biggest threat to effective execution, but it can be managed through task shedding, cross-checking, and checklists.

(*continued*)

(*continued*)

7. Nameless, rankless debriefing is key to continuous improvement and closing execution gaps.
8. Incorporating lessons learned from regular root cause analysis improves performance.
9. The right execution engine will develop leaders with a bias to action and the confidence to execute.

CHAPTER 2

BASIC TRAINING: INDOCTRINATING YOUR PEOPLE WITH VALUES AND SKILLS

Amidst the smoke and flak that covered Omaha Beach on D-Day, 1944, the U.S. Army's 5th Ranger Battalion came ashore and assembled along the beachhead. In the swirl of combat, General Norman Cota came up to a group of them as he tried to move American troops inland.

"What unit are you with?" he screamed over the shells and gunfire.

"Fifth Rangers," one replied.

"Well then," the general said. "Rangers lead the way!"

And so they did, as they have ever since. When soldiers were needed to scale the rocky cliffs of Point du Hoc near Utah Beach to disable German guns, the Rangers answered the call. And, on Omaha, in the darkest hour of the invasion, the Army's two-year-old special forces group helped lead the breakout from that deathtrap of a beach to the high ground. From D-Day forward, their battle cry has been the same: "Rangers lead the way."

Today, the Rangers are among the most respected special operations forces in the world. They've carried their combat toughness and their rallying cry into every U.S. conflict since World War II. And despite the passing years since those days on Omaha Beach, every successive generation of Rangers has had one thing in common. Every soldier who wears the arched yellow and black Ranger tab on his uniform started his journey at Fort Benning, Georgia, at the Ranger Assessment and Selection Program (RAS), or its forerunner, the Ranger Indoctrination Program. Roughly 350 to 400 airborne-qualified soldiers and officers volunteer for each new class but—get this—only 250 are left after the *fourth* day. Suffice it to say, those first four days are brutally tough. In freezing cold or 100-degree heat, they're running and climbing and counting out chin-ups and push-ups, scaling walls, and marching with full loads for 12 miles. If they fail to lead or fail to work as a team, they're out. How badly do they want it? That's the question for Day One. On the first day the cut is all about willpower and strength: a minimum of 49 push-ups in two minutes, 59 sit-ups in the same time period; six chin-ups performed from a dead-hang; and a five-mile run in 40 minutes. Then they're marched to the Combat Water Survival Assessment area where they're tested for their ability to handle water-related challenges. This is followed by a refresher training course in land navigation.

That's grueling enough—but it's only Day One.

Day Two starts at 3:30 A.M. with navigation exercises, weapons tests, communication tests, a 2.1-mile run in fatigues carrying an M4 rifle, followed by drills at the challenging Malvesti confidence course, where candidates scale walls, climb ropes, and crawl through a mess of mud and barbed wire known as the worm pit.

Day Three is just as tough, and then comes Day Four. On the last day, Day Four, students tackle a 12-mile march without water, carrying an average of 35 pounds each. Almost half are now gone. Those who survived are exhausted, but they're well on their way to becoming U.S. Army Rangers. The remaining phases include rock climbing and rappelling exercises in the mountains of northern Georgia, and navigation and land tactics in Florida swamps, all coupled with intense training, little sleep, and further indoctrination in survival and combat skills. By the end of it all, it's not unusual to discover that you've lost 30 pounds.

But there is so much to be proud of. After months of Ranger training, the ones still around have a mental and physical toughness that's second to none. These men have faced adversity and stared it down. They've kept marching when their energy seemed entirely gone; they've made their bodies forget hunger to get through another round of push-ups; and they've had the courage to make difficult decisions and stick by them.

And that's just what the Rangers are getting, too. In addition to the physical portion, this training process hones five key elements that the Army deems essential for its special operations forces: intelligence, mental toughness, personal courage, motivation, and discipline.[1] These aren't unlike the qualities needed in competitive business.

First, Rangers must be smart. To fight and survive in a complex world, elite soldiers must think creatively, assess situations rapidly and

---

[1]James Carabello, Command Sergeant Major, U.S. Army. Interview by author, August 8, 2013.

holistically, and act in alignment with their organization's overall mission. This can be nuanced. A Ranger can draw on all of his operational combat skills but often needs to know when to stop acting like a warrior and become a diplomat or humanitarian. Warfare is unpredictable and asymmetrical; frontline troops have to think on their feet and make decisions quickly, even in the midst of wholly unfamiliar situations.

Second, there's that mental toughness. People often forget how important mental toughness is for leaders. Not only do they have to survive in difficult circumstances, they have to make on-the-spot judgment calls in situations where no perfect data exists—and they have to live with their decisions and the consequences. Only good training and a structured decision-making process gives them that ability. Rangers come away with the courage to make those decisions and the confidence to stick to them. Said Fort Benning's Command Sergeant Major James Carabello, "The hardest part of Ranger School is being a master at every individual task, and having the physical and mental preparation to endure long hours of physically tough missions under stressful conditions. Ranger training puts you in the toughest environments, but you're still expected to perform and execute missions. As a Ranger, you'll always be held to a higher standard. You must be a leader."[2]

Third, Rangers learn courage. They develop that vitally important courage to execute we've talked about—but remember, courage is not bravado. Courage is the confidence to act that comes from preparation. During Ranger training, candidates overcome challenges and learn to rely on their team; that develops confidence. They're confronting the most difficult tasks and decisions imaginable but they're learning they can get through it. Confidence swells. When they fail, their instructors examine their mistakes and help them improve so they'll be ready for the battlefield. As confidence grows, so does the courage to act. It only builds with each personal triumph. Pretty soon it's not courage, it's just execution. By that time, a Ranger is doing things that he never imagined three months before. Confidence leads to courage, no other way to say it.

---

[2]Ibid.

Motivation, too, is vital to a Ranger. Elite military professionals are men and women of action. They are proactive. They're leaning-forward people who like to take the initiative. If they're reactive, they'll lose the fight. Rather, they are driven to act, to get ahead of the situation. They're compelled to make decisions and intuitively do the hard work necessary for victory. Nobody survives the first week of training without motivation; you don't even *sign up* for the Rangers without a heck of a lot of motivation. Only the toughest can maintain that motivation over weeks and weeks.

But then something happens. As candidates overcome obstacle after obstacle, their motivation doesn't dwindle; it doesn't tire the way their body tires. Their brains work differently. Success breeds success and their motivation burgeons. Their belief in themselves and their teams grows with each and every goal achieved.

Are you seeing a pattern here? Can you see yourself in this yet? It's the *system* that's developing winners. That's right. Winners are made, not born. Wining attitudes are gained, not inherited; earned, not given. Becoming a winner—an elite soldier, a great salesman or athlete, you name it—has little to do with that pedigree mentioned earlier. It has everything to do with the *process* to which you commit.

Perhaps above all, Rangers value discipline, and Ranger Regiments display a discipline unlike anything you're ever seen. You can hear it every time they belt out the Ranger Creed and you can see it in their actions. Discipline is part of their organizational identity. Units that lack discipline react slowly on the battlefield, get distracted, and fail to achieve their objectives. Rangers won't let that happen. And that's the next secret they have to share with us.

ORGANIZATIONAL IDENTITY AND IMPERATIVES

As raw soldiers morph into Rangers, they become something other than soldiers or individuals—they become a team of soldiers called Rangers and they get a sense of who they are and what they're a part of. As their training progresses, those who don't wash out begin learning the Ranger Creed and become indoctrinated in the *culture* of the Army Rangers.

"You have to live by the Ranger Creed," explained Command Sergeant Major Carabello. "Not only do you have army values, you have the Ranger Creed. And that's drilled into your head each and every day. It's not just knowing the words, it's *living* the words. It's something you apply to what you do every day. If you are a Ranger in the Ranger Regiment, you will always remember the creed. It influences your entire life."

Here it is:

Recognizing that I volunteered as a Ranger, fully knowing the hazards of my chosen profession, I will always endeavor to uphold the prestige, honor, and high esprit de corps of my Ranger Regiment.

Acknowledging the fact that a Ranger is a more elite soldier who arrives at the cutting edge of battle by land, sea, or air, I accept the fact that as a Ranger my country expects me to move further, faster, and fight harder than any other soldier.

Never shall I fail my comrades. I will always keep myself mentally alert, physically strong, and morally straight, and I will shoulder more than my share of the task, whatever it may be, 100 percent and then some.

Gallantly will I show the world that I am a specially-selected and well-trained soldier. My courtesy to superior officers, neatness of dress, and care of equipment shall set the example for others to follow.

Energetically will I meet the enemies of my country. I shall defeat them on the field of battle for I am better trained and will fight with all my might. Surrender is not a Ranger word. I will never leave a fallen comrade to fall into the hands of the enemy and under no circumstances will I ever embarrass my country.

Readily will I display the intestinal fortitude required to fight on to the Ranger objective and complete the mission, though I be the lone survivor.

The Ranger Creed spells out the organizational identity of this elite unit. During physical training (PT), it's not uncommon for drill instructors to pull candidates to their feet and make them recite the parts of the creed, which builds on the army's seven core values. Listen to the drill instructors. They'll yell out these words:

1. Loyalty
2. Duty
3. Respect
4. Selfless service
5. Honor
6. Integrity
7. Personal courage

Together, the army's core values and the Ranger Creed create a unique organizational identity that breeds unity and trust. This is the glue that holds everything together. Rangers are expected to do their best and meet a higher standard. And in the field, they're able to execute at high levels because their unit is infused with trust. They have clear, common goals, and they know every man on their team has endured the same tests, the same training, the same experiences. They can trust each other to execute and be adaptive, agile soldiers, and achieve their common objective. If a soldier isn't committed to his profession, to being a Ranger, he won't make it, and it's no different in business. Identity is the system of mirrors that focus the attributes of the process into a laser beam of energy that's aligned behind the company and its mission. Rangers are dedicated to being Rangers. And IBMers? You get the idea. These teams have their identity and they are driven to embrace it.

But, to repeat, none of this is a birthright. It's a process. The military focuses less on recruiting the right people and more on delivering the right training. Certainly, new servicemen and women need basic qualifications and a disposition to serve just as any corporate employee would, but through its highly developed training process, the military knows it can shape a broad range of people into modern warriors, some of whom will become truly elite, like the Rangers. Through this exacting training, Rangers learn those qualities that define their unit, those powerful attributes that remain unchanging: their identity, their purpose, the guidelines for their behavior. When new Rangers receive their yellow and black tabs, they have no doubt about their organizational imperative—their reason for being.

Successful organizations are like that, too. I know because I've seen it in the military and in the civilian world. Almost without fail, everyone in a successful organization displays these very same Ranger traits, and most importantly, everyone has this clear understanding of their reason for being. They know their purpose, they have a set of values, a mission, a process; they want to serve customers or constituents, or to create wealth. Moreover, the organization has the ability to focus and execute according to this purpose, and they perpetuate this sense of dedication from the bottom up.

Take Southwest Airlines. Southwest occupies a top spot on most customer satisfaction lists, even though it competes in an industry that is, by nature, a minefield of customer problems: weather delays, mechanical issues, luggage problems. Yet despite their high customer rankings, Southwest's focus isn't their customers, rather, they focus on their employees, their "beLUVed employees," as they say, referencing the symbol for their stock—LUV—which goes back to their home airport, Love Field in Dallas, Texas, and their first advertising campaigns.

On Valentine's Day each year, the company stages an elaborate ceremony to award their Heroes of the Heart award. The award is bestowed upon a team of Southwest employees who don't even interact with customers, a group of hard-working but low-profile employees who are often overlooked but who are essential to the running of an airline. Southwest makes sure they're rewarded in a high-profile way; the winning department's name is emblazoned beside the Heroes of the Heart logo on one of the fleet's airplanes.[3]

Let's dig deeper, because it goes deeper. If you examine the company's strategic initiatives you will see that again they revolve

---

[3]Southwest Airlines, "2010 One Report: Employee Engagement and Recognition," August 5, 2013. www.southwestonereport.com/people_em_eng.php.

around employees. One of those is the Kick Tail program. Kick Tail is designed to encourage employees to help Southwest become:

1. #1 in low costs with our warrior spirits.
2. #1 in customer satisfaction with our servant's hearts.
3. #1 in employee SPIRIT with our fun-LUVing attitudes.

When employees observe others doing great work to support those goals, they'll send Kick Tail-A-Grams. The recipients become eligible for prizes, and Southwest allocates $1 million each year for the program. That becomes a powerful motivator and a highly effective way to build an organizational identity and a strong, unique culture.[4]

So why employees first? Why this dedication to each other, this Ranger-like focus on their identity? Southwest puts its employees first, believing that happy employees create happy customers. Happy customers, in turn, create profits and shareholder value. It turns out that Southwest is right. Its stock has nearly tripled in value over the past four years, and before the mega-mergers of Delta and Northwest, and United and Continental, Southwest carried more passengers within the United States than any other airline. Today it ranks third and proudly touts its unique brand, culture, and customer following. And if you've flown Southwest as often as I have, you've experienced the LUV too.

But let's go on. In addition to their organizational imperative, corporations, like military units, instill their people with a belief in their principles. Principles are cardinal rules so important to your organization that they should never be broken. They are things you *always* do or *never* do. They are your guardrails.

Let's go back to Southwest and the airline's three goals, which help define what they call the Southwest Way. Southwest wants you to have a warrior's spirit, a servant's heart, and a fun-LUVing attitude. To help employees understand how they're supposed to act, Southwest translated these three goals into defined guidelines, organizational imperatives, if you will.

---

[4]Ibid.

The Warrior Spirit means Southwest employees should always:

1. Work hard.
2. Desire to be the best.
3. Be courageous.
4. Display urgency.
5. Persevere.
6. Innovate.

To exhibit a Servant's Heart, employees should:

1. Follow the Golden Rule.
2. Adhere to the organization's principles.
3. Treat others with respect.
4. Put others first.
5. Be egalitarian.
6. Demonstrate proactive customer service.
7. Embrace the Southwest family.

When exhibiting the fun-LUVing attitude to customers and each other, employees should:

1. Have fun.
2. Not take themselves too seriously.
3. Maintain perspective.
4. Celebrate success.
5. Enjoy their work.
6. Be passionate team players.

Each Southwest employee knows without a doubt whether he or she fits in at Southwest. The company has given them a clear vision and a set of measures to guide their actions. They have an identity with guardrails to show the boundaries. Simple. Easy to understand. Companywide.[5]

---

[5] Ibid.

Trader Joe's is like that, too. Like Southwest, they have a clear organizational identity and use it to create a powerful driver for their own success. The company began in California as a friendly, neighborhood grocery store and, as it expanded across the country, management didn't want to lose that feel. Crew members, Trader Joe's name for employees, are brought in and imbued with the company culture and identity. They receive lessons in leadership and teamwork; they learn about every product they sell. They wear Hawaiian shirts and casual attire to create a relaxed, adventurous, and fun shopping environment. They learn to multitask, meaning they share responsibilities in stocking shelves, selecting products, answering questions, operating checkout lanes, and being general ambassadors. About their products, they say, "We tried it. We like it. If you don't, bring it back for a refund or exchange—no hassles."[6] Trader Joe's employees stand behind that policy and are empowered to take care of their customers. They learn teamwork, and work in a team atmosphere that in turn creates real attachment. Evidence of that? The company's employee turnover rate is only 4 percent—far below the national average for grocers.

We know the rest of the story. When a Trader Joe's comes to town, the parking lots around it fill up quickly and stay packed. The overall approach pleases their customers, builds relationships, and lets the company accomplish its mission. They *are* a local grocer. They *are* a fun place to shop. National chain? Maybe, but you're hard-pressed to tell. Their uniquely strong corporate culture makes every store's culture feel special. Through its employees, products, and the personal shopping experience it provides, Trader Joe's stores have created their unique identity, fortified their niche and, as a result, generated exceptional growth. One study conducted on Trader Joe's found that the overarching culture of teamwork and direct participation created an environment that bred particularly high performance and collaboration. That translated directly to the dedicated customer orientation that makes the chain so successful. How successful? The privately-held company, founded in 1967, operates more than 400 stores and grosses

---

[6]Trader Joe's "About Us," (n.d.) www.traderjoes.com/about/index.

roughly $8 billion in revenue each year. Those stores produce $1,750 in sales per square foot, among the highest yields in the industry. By comparison, Whole Foods stores yield half as much.[7] That's the power of strong organizational identity. It aligns everyone to a common set of values that are planks to the company's overall mission. That identity radiates outward, engaging and converting the customers in a positive way. Whether you're in the airline, grocery, or national defense business, your success depends on your people having it.

In the end, it's just the same as the Ranger *esprit de corps*.

THE TRAINING IMPERATIVE

Once an organization clearly establishes its identity and instills the related principles in its employees or members, it must begin to prepare its people to execute its mission. Here we have new examples to draw upon; let's look at aircraft carriers. Few environments are more dangerous and more challenging than the deck of a modern U.S. aircraft carrier. At first glance, a flight deck seems entirely chaotic and noisy, full of visual distractions like steam, aircraft, and men running. It's the type of place where a green airman might cause himself serious harm or easily get someone else hurt. Props and rotors are cranking, jets are landing and launching, and people and aircraft are constantly moving.

So how does it work? How do those green airmen and sailors thrive and survive to become veterans?

The flight deck of a carrier is in fact a major airport wedged onto a deck of steel four-and-a-half acres in size run by a cast of hundreds, the average age of whom is around 20 years old. Many are on their first cruise; some have never seen a F/A-18E Super Hornet before. But now those jets are all around them with afterburners roaring only feet from their faces. Chaotic? At first glance, yes. On second glance, not at all. Few places are more carefully organized.

---

[7]Beth Kowitt, "Inside the Secret World of Trader Joe's," *Fortune*, August 23, 2010. http://money.cnn.com/2010/08/20/news/companies/inside_trader_joes_full_version.fortune/index.htm.

Flight deck operations work because of training that starts at the Naval Air Technical Training Center (NATTC) in Pensacola, Florida. When trainees arrive, they're fresh from basic training and ready to learn specific skills. At NATTC, they get just that. They'll learn to repair engines at sea, fight fires, refuel planes; they'll learn how to preflight a helicopter, a jet, a cargo plane, or how to load ordnance. When they graduate, they're beginning to make some sense of it all.

From here they go to the fleet where they'll be mentored and trained on the job by experienced deck hands. The military doesn't expect its neophytes to do everything correctly at first, so they've implemented an apprentice system that's world-class. Seniors are always training juniors. Success follows success and the trainees grow in confidence. A sense of team identity emerges and that feeling of confidence takes hold. The insecurity and confusion of nine months ago is forgotten in the roar of jets and pride of jobs well done.

It is the process, of course, that breeds confidence and creates a bias toward accountable action. The process gives the sailor the courage to step into that dangerous environment and execute. A new Ranger may have never been in a firefight, but his training has prepared him so well that he might as well be a combat veteran. He knows exactly what to do and how to react.

Can you see where this fits in? By going through a regimented process, you develop people who have the tools they need to convert a confusing and intimidating business environment into one where people move about with carrier deck precision and Ranger confidence. Imagine putting five people on the front desk of a Marriott hotel without the right training, or training them in the rote functions of data entry without explaining the layout of the rooms in the hotel. Many companies hesitate to invest in training, often because of the cost. But at the same time, they often feel like they can't compete without that level of training. Guess which side of that coin wins.

At my company, Afterburner, every time I begin a training session, I start with learning objectives. I always state the desired learning objective (DLO). If I don't state my DLO, the training won't be focused and my student won't completely understand what he or she is supposed to learn. At the end of the session, I test out the DLOs. Did they achieve my objectives for the training? Did the training succeed? I test and verify, like I did so many times in the air force.

The military's elite teams train incessantly. The training starts out with an intense, concentrated program, often focusing on simple execution. The teams don't learn from fancy models or complex processes. They do, repeat, and improve. But training doesn't end there. It goes on as long as you're in the service. We never cease training, never cease honing our skills—and we happily pass those skills to the ones coming along behind us. When they have a mission, they're ready to go.

In April 2009, Somali pirates attacked the cargo ship *Maersk Alabama* in the Indian Ocean off the Horn of Africa. After a fight with the ship's determined crew, four pirates escaped into a lifeboat with a hostage, the captain. They headed for shore to start the ransom process. They didn't get far in the rough seas with limited fuel, however, and a tense five-day standoff began. Unfortunately for the pirates, those five days gave an elite team of navy snipers time to fly to the destroyer USS *Bainbridge*, which was tracking the pirates and their hostage captain.

Let me tell you about SEAL snipers. These guys rank among the best sharpshooters in the world. They start on the range like any soldier but then they learn to shoot at ultralong distances or from unstable platforms. They take surgical shots from helicopters, boats, vehicles—anything. The sniper program has exacting standards and even trained SEALs will wash out. It's an elite group within an elite group, and for good reason. On the drop of a dime, these men may one day have to execute in near-impossible conditions and lives may depend on their precision.

So it was during the *Maersk Alabama* incident. The Indian Ocean soon grew rougher, and the lifeboat with the pirates and their hostage ran out of fuel. The captain of the *Bainbridge* persuaded the pirates to let the navy tow them. A tow line was tossed, the lifeboat was hooked to it, and the sniper mission was now a go. Once *Bainbridge* began towing the lifeboat, three SEAL snipers positioned themselves near the ship's stern to take out the three pirates if the hostage's life appeared endangered. They and their spotters gauged the range, checked the wind, picked their targets, and waited. They watched the lifeboat roll and pitch in the waves. They knew their business. They were trained in low light and with night-vision scopes. They were trained to hit small targets at a range of 100 yards, the exact same length of the tow rope (which was no coincidence). They were prepared, and they were confident.

They waited.

When the captain's life was judged to be in jeopardy, the *Bainbridge* quietly inserted several swimmers into the water and ordered them to approach the lifeboat and await the snipers' action. It was now near dusk. The snipers calculated the motion of the lifeboat, the pitch and roll of the destroyer. The spotters waited. Finally, the order was passed down to execute the mission. Over their headsets, all three sniper heard the same thing: "Three, two, one, execute, execute, execute!" *Blink*. It was over. Bad guys down, captain saved.[8]

That's training.

Can you imagine a technology company like Google or Facebook or Amazon without a go-team of highly trained, always-ready, ultra-talented specialists ready to deploy at the first sign of a system failure? No. Every organization has its snipers, its trained specialists. The mission to safely recover the hostage was successful because the snipers had trained relentlessly and executed flawlessly. When they lined up for their shots, they didn't do anything haphazardly. They followed a carefully designed process that gave them the best opportunity to succeed; training and good process eliminate variables.

That's what good training gets you: specialists who can execute.

The path to success is no different in business.

---

[8]Chris Hogerman, "Navy SEALs Hunting at Sea," April 7, 2013. http://navyseals .com/2186/navy-seals-hunting-at-sea/.

THE TRUST IMPERATIVE

When the three snipers on the *Bainbridge* got ready to fire, they each knew how the others would breathe, think, and react. Moreover, they knew who would target which pirate, and that all of them would pull their triggers at the same instant, eliminating any possible retaliation against the hostage. It had to be that way. If they got it wrong, a life was at stake. But they didn't. Without speaking a word, they squeezed their triggers as one. That's trust. And guess what? If a team doesn't build trust, a team falls apart. And just like you can train courage, you can train trust.

A high-stakes environment forges trust like nothing else. So let's shift gears and look at a group of aviators whose trust is so explicit that they're willing to fly $30 million supersonic fighter jets at 400 miles per hour with just inches between their wings. I'm talking about the elite group of aviation personnel who join the Blue Angels, the U.S. Navy's flight demonstration squadron. Millions of spectators the world over have seen them fly the Blue Angel delta formation, made up of all six aircraft, and the Blue Angel diamond, which involves the number one through four jets. In the diamond, those four aircraft are tucked together so tightly that, at times, only 18 inches separate cockpits and wingtips. The four jets climb and turn and maintain that close formation through a series of breathtaking maneuvers—and they do it without looking ahead. Yep. The pilots stay in position not by looking ahead but by looking to the side or above, at particular points on the aircraft next to them. It's called "flying the paint."

Often only *the Boss*, the commanding officer flying Blue Angel One, watches the ground. If the Boss flies too close to the trees, then the whole formation will follow him because they're not looking ahead at all, just at him or the paint on the closest jet.

To maintain such focus and ignore the hazards around them, Blue Angels Two, Three, and Four have implicit and total trust in the Boss. The other three pilots rely entirely on him to fly the diamond safely along their prebriefed course. If they're in a steep dive, they trust the Boss to pull up before they get too low; they're solely focused on maintaining their position *vis-à-vis* the other aircraft. If one jet falls out of formation, the entire group breaks up or worse. But such negative thoughts don't exist inside those four cockpits. Preparation and trust have vanquished doubts, mistrust, and hesitancy. Trust is the essential ingredient. Trust is what makes formation flight work.

Not all the Blue Angels fly the diamond. While their four diamond brethren are flying their tight formation, Blue Angels Five and Six gallivant around the sky, demonstrating the maximum capabilities of the F/A-18 Hornet. They hit the afterburners, and push the speed to the limits. They turn and bank and spiral up into the sky. But the maneuver that always gets the crowd to its feet is their inverted-to-inverted pass—a high-speed, low-altitude head-on pass flown entirely upside down. Few maneuvers prove more demanding.

To pull it off, Blue Angels Five and Six face off against one another, six miles apart, each three miles from the show's center. Now, at six miles, neither of the pilots can see the other; they're just specks in the distance. Facing each other, they push the throttles forward and start screaming toward show center at the rate of one mile per eight seconds. When they're three miles apart, they roll over and go upside down. To the crowd, it appears they're on a collision course, inverted. Even though they're exceptionally trained, it's a difficult maneuver. They have to align themselves so precisely that a mistake of just a few feet could send them into an actual head-on collision. But there's trust. Both aviators trust their opposite to be exactly where he was briefed to be regarding airspeed, altitude, and position over the field. So into the center they scream, inverted at 460 miles per hour, a mere 200 feet above the ground. Just before they meet, Blue Angel Five calls, "Ready, hit it!" They each push the stick left and roll 360-degrees back to inverted. The crowd gasps, then cheers. The two jets pass without touching, their wingtips just yards apart. They fly down the runway, then climb into the sky, still upside down.

The applause is deafening. *What a close call.* But to the Blue Angels it's just another air show. What the crowd doesn't realize is that these aviators will fly that exact maneuver hundreds of times during a season. And before that, hundreds more in off-season training. It's not raw talent or luck. It's not present from birth. It's a process. It's training. The on-boarding and training process used by the Blue Angels gives new team members the skill and courage to execute the inverted-to-inverted pass just like it gave the SEAL snipers the skill and courage to free the captain of *Maersk Alabama*. None of these flyers began their careers able to perform the pass or the squadron's other aerobatics. They're only able to fly these maneuvers because a proven process replaced fear with trust, inadequacy with preparation. They hold every team member to a very high yet achievable standard, which drives both team and organizational accountability. Nothing is more important. In this business, pilots can't hide behind excuses, and there can be a prohibitively high cost of not doing a job properly. You can bet that accountability is crucial.

The Blue Angels' chain of trust extends well beyond the flyers in the cockpit. At the beginning of each show, the pilots climb into their jets, trusting that their crew chief has the aircraft in perfect condition. They trust a young man or woman, usually under 30 years of age and without a college degree, to have their jet preflighted, to have the right switches at the correct positions, and to have every part and wire in the aircraft in top shape (and these are the oldest F/A-18s in the fleet, many older than their maintainers and pilots). Maintenance crews know they're accountable and can spend entire nights repairing or simply checking the smallest pieces of an engine or landing gear. They know the pilot trusts them to ensure that the plane will carry him safely through his flight and back home again.

As you can imagine, this generates some repartee between these pilots and their maintainers. The crew chiefs often say to pilots, "Don't break my aircraft, sir." The pilots smile knowingly. It's just what they want to hear. The maintainers consider the aircraft theirs; they take care of them diligently. They just let the aviators borrow them.

Trust is indeed a circle. Effective leaders understand this and create a culture that nurtures a sense of trust. A brilliant strategy injected into the wrong environment will fail. Bad culture can torpedo even the best strategies. Doubt, worry—these are the enemies of execution. Successful companies combat them by building processes to create trust.

Trust enables open communication, and that's particularly important during the planning process. Trust enables teamwork and alignment, and that's integral to the execution phase. And trust builds leadership, and that's key to your future. Corporate leaders must communicate a highly defined end state, a vivid destination, to their people and align their entire organization to achieve it—more on that in the next chapter.

THE LEADERSHIP IMPERATIVE

Nobody wants to ride a headless horse; every organization has a leader. But we all know that. The real question is, do you have a leadership training process? We think that's an organizational imperative too many companies overlook. And it shouldn't just be about training the C-suite. Elite military organizations have hundreds of generals, thousands of officers, and each one, in their area, is a vital, trusted leader. And they become leaders through a process, not through learning an art. Chances are, each leader started his journey through that process as a buzz-cutted recruit or cadet, nervous and at least half-scared, wondering if he or she could hack the first week in uniform.

Inprocessing Day is what the U.S. Air Force Academy calls the day new cadets first report for duty and begin that long passage to becoming leaders of men and women. A succession of cars and minivans arrive at Doolittle Hall to drop off 18-year-olds. The parents who leave their sons or daughters at the door know that it's the beginning of an experience that will transform their children in ways they can't entirely comprehend. On that day, their children begin to become warriors. On that day, they begin to become leaders.

In Doolittle Hall, upperclass cadets welcome the families and help them navigate the check-in. The parents say their final goodbyes, the new cadets file onto a waiting bus, and then it all *really* begins.

No more smiles—down to business. The academy has just four years to mold these dewy kids into officers, so the upperclass cadets unleash their infamous welcome and pointedly let new arrivals know that they're in the U.S. Air Force now. This is their new family. Mom and Dad are gone. All they have is each other; they're all in the same boat. And they have so much to learn. Someone isn't standing straight, someone is looking to the side, someone is holding a bag in the wrong hand. The upperclassmen let them know it.

"When bad coffee breath hit me, I knew this was actually happening," recalled Air Force Academy graduate Brandon Williams. "I'd apparently not been standing straight enough in formation. When the yelling started six inches from my face, I knew there was no turning back and everything had to be done *their* way."

By the day's end, all the new cadets look the same. They're wearing the same clothes and have brand-new air force haircuts. They're eating the same food, getting up at the same hour, going the same places—even their vocabulary is air force. They're allowed only seven responses to upperclassmen:

1. Yes/no, sir/ma'am.
2. No excuse, sir/ma'am.
3. Sir/ma'am, the answer is....
4. Sir/ma'am, may I ask a question?
5. Sir/ma'am, may I make a statement?
6. Sir/ma'am, I do not know. (I will find out.)
7. Sir/ma'am, I do not understand.

Culture is emerging. Identity is forming. New languages, new histories, new worlds. Every cadet lives by *Contrails*, the cadet's official handbook. Contents range from air force history to modern aircraft, from famous military quotes to how many windows the dining hall has. New cadets are responsible for knowing every bit of information in that book, and more. If an upperclass cadet shares a piece of knowledge, the cadet with whom he shares it had better tell others. "If one knows it, you all should know it," goes the saying. They're in it together. They start to know the U.S. Air Force backwards and forwards, including the all-important values: integrity first, service before self, excellence in all we do.

"You're becoming a *part* of this institution," said Williams. "And I mean the U.S. military more so than the academy per se. You're not in this for a month or a year. You're committing to a long haul so you really get vested. And everyone knows that they're starting on a long process, and over time, we'll learn the values and skills we need to lead men and women in times of war and peace."[9]

Future generals and chairmen of the Joint Chiefs of Staff started off as cadets at the service academies. They all stood and took abuse from upperclass cadets. They all learned and recited the same facts, slogans, and responses. They all became indoctrinated in the culture of America's military. Before they ever lead, they learned to follow.

Look at your own training programs. Are you developing leaders? Is there a place where you can afford *not* to have leaders? Probably not. So don't just think of the C-suite when you think of leadership. The military puts its new people into a process that will make them into leaders step-by-step, at every level. Developing leaders is an imperative; the military knows this and we should, too. Every organization needs a pipeline that steadily produces the next leaders. You start filling that pipeline by defining and creating a deliberate leadership development *process*.

(In the last section of each chapter to come, we'll track our elite warriors as they become capable team members and high-performing leaders.)

MISSION CHECKLIST

Effective Organizations:
1. Create a defined organizational identity.
2. Drive identity and organizational imperatives through their ranks.
3. Define guidelines for behavior.
4. Know why—for what purpose—they exist.
5. Relentlessly focus on that purpose.

---

[9]Brandon Williams. Interview by author, August 12, 2013.

6. Create a defined organizational identity.
7. Drive identity, common values, and organizational imperatives through their ranks.
8. Define guidelines for behavior.
9. Adopt training programs that support their purpose and identity.
10. Build trust through mutual accountability.

CHAPTER 3

TEAM ALIGNMENT: CONNECTING THE TROOPS WITH THE LEADER'S INTENT

Once we've onboarded our people, gotten them steeped in identity, culture, and skills, we begin the subtle but crucial process of aligning them to our goals. And that takes building their trust. Not the trust they have in one another—rather, I'm asking them to trust me. No one trusts out of the blue, but ultimately, everyone wants to have confidence in the person in charge. So to align people, you first get in sync with your environment and *their* environment. Get in step with the up-to-the-minute data, and then articulate a clear vision of where you want to take your troops. Let's look at another example.

Not to be outdone by their navy brethren in the Blue Angels, the U.S. Marine Corps has its own elite showmen. Perhaps the most famous group is the Silent Drill Platoon: 24 marines who have an exceptional organizational identity, a clear mission, and who personify coordination and synchronicity. They are known for flawlessly executing rifle drills without speaking a word or relying on any other cues. (You can get a glimpse of them in action in the opening credits of the film *A Few Good Men*.) The platoon spends about 140 days on the road each year, and 10 to 12 hours of drilling per day is common.

So what can we learn from them? Clad in dark-blue tunics with gold buttons, white trousers, polished shoes, white gloves, and white hats with stern black brims, these marines march into an arena in tight formation, carrying rifles with fixed bayonets. The platoon steps in unison, then performs a series of drills where every move is in perfect sync with the others. The marines' gloved hands and shined shoes move at the same instant, twirling rifles and marching in precise cadence. Nothing demonstrates their coordination better than when they line up shoulder to shoulder and drill with their rifles. Their line is arrow-straight. They execute their movements precisely. When the marines unshoulder their rifles milliseconds apart it seem like a waterfall of rifles that moves left to right in a visually-stunning feat of discipline. These men know coordination.

The marines selected for the Silent Drill Platoon appreciate the honor and the opportunity to join such a special fraternity but at the end of their tour, they all readily rejoin their fellow marines in the field. In the field, planning and execution look different from a drill practice or at a performance before a stadium crowd of 50,000, but it still demands coordination. In military or business combat, coordination is indispensable, and it starts with being in tune with your environment.

Whether it's in an arena performing before 50,000 or in the field with a team of two, we call this being-in-tune SA—Situational Awareness. Having it is the first step in aligning your people to your goals.

SITUATIONAL AWARENESS

It's all well and good to be an elite soldier imbued with confidence, courage, motivation, and trust, but it takes even more to survive on the battlefield. It starts with Situational Awareness. Every time I step into the cockpit of my jet, I'm hyperaware of *everything* around me because everything around me affects my mission. I know my terrain, I know what's over the next hill, I know where the good guys are and where the bad guys are supposed to be; I know how high the mountains are and what rivers cross my flight path. One glance at the sky and I know my weather, too, and I'll look at the brief to see what it's like over the target. I know where I'm headed, how I want to get there, what I'm supposed to do at the objective, and how I'm going to get back. SA right from the start. That's the big picture.

Then fresh data starts to flow. At takeoff, I worry about crisp communications, the position of other aircraft, birds, and the immediate weather. Aloft, I have to stay within a specified airspace, remain on a specified course, avoid other aircraft, watch my fuel, track targets on my radar, and employ the right weapons at the right time. And there are other complicating factors that I have to look out for: clouds, darkness, bogeys, and threats to my mission like surface-to-air missiles. I never let down my guard; I have to stay on top of everything.

Thankfully, I'm awash in good data streaming to me while I fly my mission. On my instrument panel I have an altitude indicator, an airspeed indicator, a rate of climb or descent indicator, a heading indicator, radar, and more. I have audio tones coming through my helmet and new data flashing up on my Heads Up Display. Every bit of it makes sense and keeps me on top of the situation.

Same for Delta Force, SEALs, and Rangers. They roger up with night vision goggles, laser scopes, and comm links. Mutually supporting teams feed each other situational data on the ground. Data inputs keep us all on track, keep us ahead of our problems, help us stay proactive. Through it all there is one set of data that is paramount to me as a pilot. Inside my cockpit I have one utterly vital indicator with the metrics that sums it up best. It's called the attitude indicator. It sits in the middle of my display panels and shows the aircraft's position relative to the horizon. A blue area indicates sky, a white line denotes the horizon, and brown indicates the ground. If the indicator shows mostly blue, the houses below are getting smaller and my aircraft is climbing. If it shows mostly brown, the houses are getting bigger, which means I'm descending toward the ground. During flight, pilots constantly check our instruments and that begins and ends with the attitude indicator. We check our airspeed, then attitude. We check our fuel, then back to attitude. We check our heading, then attitude. It's called crosschecking, a hub-and-spoke approach that keeps the aircraft on the right track, keeps us aware of exactly where we are.

Now add the stress of combat. Fighter pilots have a saying: "Lose sight, lose the fight." In a real air-to-air scenario, only one aircraft is going home. We can never stop monitoring our instruments, but in a dogfight we've got to keep an eye on our adversary—the bandit. That adds one more burden. Eyes inside the cockpit; eyes out. Fly the jet, watch the bogey. All the while you're dealing with g-forces that can make a 200-pound pilot weigh 1,600 pounds. Flying gets complicated and it can be tough to stay focused. Even when tracking a bandit, we can't afford to take our eye off the enemy for more than a second, but the attitude indicator will help us know where we are in relation to our biggest threat: the ground.

You need gauges. You need data. You need situational awareness. Interesting thing, it's all around you. Like pilots, businesspeople have to understand the environment they're operating in, and how that environment is evolving and changing over time. Without situational awareness—without understanding your environment and the conditions affecting it—you're two steps behind the competition. Without SA you simply can't be aligned with other units or the overarching mission of your company. Nor can you achieve your individual goals. How do you know what to do if you don't know where you are, where you're headed, and what factors or variables could wreck your plans?

Thankfully, business has its own attitude indicator. It's called STEEP, five key categories of information that you always come back to as you implement your plans. Here they are:

1. **S**ocial: consumer attitudes, societal trends, public interests and concerns.
2. **T**echnological: changing and emerging technology, new capabilities, new collaborative opportunities, new systems and markets.
3. **E**conomic: regional and global economies, broader economic systems and trends.
4. **E**nvironmental: ecological or geological events and trends, weather, natural resources.
5. **P**olitical: legislation, regulation, liability, business climate.

I've seen companies try to compete using the same strategies that worked for them before the 2008 downturn. Their executives holed themselves up in their offices, creating a strategy for 2017 based on the 2007 environment. Well, what should their "Economic" indicator tell them? They may desperately want those old times to return, but if they don't consider how things have changed, they're sunk. They'll pump resources into a strategy that's doomed to fail because they haven't properly assessed social, technological, economic, environmental, and political realities. Their pricing and positioning will be wrong, and every frontline worker will know the plan is doomed and that senior management just doesn't understand the reality of the current business environment. STEEP is the solution. You have to consider your environment so you can align with reality and where you are. Only then will your troops trust you. Building organization-level situational awareness means you're creating a future based on real conditions. If your plans aren't grounded in reality, believe me, your troops will know it and your plans will fail. As we near the planning process, we must first grasp the reality of our current situation.

Situational awareness is the cornerstone in aligning a company, and it can be global, regional, or market-specific. One former member of the army's vaunted 160th Special Operations Aviation Regiment, the Night Stalkers, left the high-stakes special operations realm and began working for Boston Scientific, a cutting-edge technology company that had expanded into medical devices. He had no corporate or medical experience, but was immediately tasked with integrating four major business units: interventional cardiology, peripheral intervention, customer relationship management (CRM), and electrophysiology. He entered a completely unfamiliar environment, so he did what was natural to him—he built situational awareness quickly so he could accomplish his tasks and ensure that the people working under him had confidence in his leadership and judgment.

Being a pilot, he re-created his cockpit. He designed dashboards of metrics that would instantly convey the current health of each business unit and track its progress along the integration timeline. He constantly updated his dashboard and dispersed the information to his team leads to facilitate their engagement and increase their confidence in him. He used measures like attrition to determine whether employees were hearing management's positive message about integration, or if competitors were poaching top employees who worried about their future at the company. He used profit and loss statements from individual offices to determine where to consolidate or reduce. He tracked the ratio of administrative support staff to salespeople to ensure his field teams could focus on selling. If the ratio grew too large, that automatically triggered the hiring of more support staff. As he learned in the military, he never focused on one metric to the neglect of others. He used that hub-and-spoke model and always kept track of the most important measures. He never lost sight of his business's current position or where it was headed. Like an elite warrior, he gained and maintained situational awareness for himself and for his team so they could all meet their two-year timelines. Eventually, he would oversee a sales force of 1,600 professionals. In the end, thanks to maintaining hyper-SA, Boston Scientific and our special operator completed the integration in 14 months—10 months ahead of schedule.

Sometimes, however, it's difficult to trust your data. You may see trends or hear reports that cause you to question your strategy or your operational plans. The hype surrounding new technology or new trends may tempt you to change plans when, in fact, your data may suggest you stay the course. If you've done your homework in developing and measuring your metrics, trust the data.

In 2010, my sister, Captain Cheryl Murphy, was flying a C-130 Hercules cargo plane to replenish a unit of marines embedded deep within Afghanistan's Hindu Kush Mountains. As night fell, the flying became particularly treacherous. The terrain below was completely dark, entirely devoid of lights for visual references. She flew on, trusting her instruments, until she saw infrared markers lining the makeshift runway laid out by the marines. She began descending in a tight spiral to minimize her exposure to any Taliban rockets and to stay safely between mountain peaks. She checked her instruments and was still on course, but as she lined up for her final approach, her copilot pointed out they were misaligned with the runway. She checked her instruments; the instruments told her the aircraft was still on course. Concerned, she looked through her night vision goggles and, sure enough, she saw the avenue of glowing infrared markers at an angle to her approach. It looked as if she was off course, that she needed to come right 30 degrees. She began to push the big aircraft right, then stopped. Her training would not let her ignore her navigational data. Always trust your instruments. She pulled back hard on the yoke, pushed up the throttles, and took the big Hercules back into the sky.

She made the right call. When she contacted the marines on the ground, they discovered another aircraft had blown the infrared markers out of position. Her instruments had, in fact, been correct. Had she trusted her eyes and the out-of-position lights, she would have flown the C-130 into the mountain. Learn to trust your key indicators.

HIGH-DEFINITION DESTINATION
AND LEADER'S INTENT

Once you have situational awareness and are aligned with reality, planners can begin crafting *strategy*. That process begins by answering four questions:

1. Who are we (our organizational identity)?
2. Where are we (our situational awareness)?
3. Where are we going (our high-definition destination, or HDD)?
4. How do we get there (our strategy)?

At this point in our process, we should understand the first two points—who we are and where we are. We know our identity, we've trained to be who we are, and we have people on our teams who trust one another. We know where we are—our SA is high and our data inputs have us alert, centered, and in the present. The bigger questions now become "Where are we going?" and "What will it look like when we get there?"

At the outset of any strategy process, a business organization must determine where it wants to go, what it wants to accomplish, and how it plans to set itself apart from others in the marketplace. The big "hows" and "whats" are now front and center: How will you be different, what will you look like three years from now, and how will you operate in your desired future state? Note I say "future state," not vision. This future state isn't a "vision." Vision is about the big picture, the general idea. Vision often gets muddied into vague aspirations or lofty goals, ivory tower ideas. That might have worked a generation ago, but today's world is too complex and too rapidly changing for generalities and ambiguities. Your people need to know specifics so they can react quickly and correctly.

Now, we're talking about a modern, high-definition picture of your future state, a real 1080p image of where we're going, something we call our high-definition destination (HDD). You know what high def is. Grainy black-and-white television sets won't cut it any more than a few generalized words will in a business strategy. Think exclusively in high definition and create a specific, detailed, granular, crystal-clear picture of what you'll look like and how you'll be operating when your organization reaches its intended future destination. You can zoom in on any part of it and it's still crystal clear. You can see detail. In fact, it's so clear that everyone gets the picture of where the company is going. It can drive specific actions and measures, so that the organization's plans, checkpoints, and goals are all clearly aligned.

Effective leaders will start by designing a HDD that all in their organization can envision and they'll do it in enough detail so everyone can understand the precise actions needed to get there. When that happens, troops and leadership are in alignment because they can all envision the same future destination and how they individually contribute to reaching it. Each person can function with near-perfect precision within the team structure; everyone at every level is capable of making decisions that support the goals of their unit, team, squadron, company, or battalion. They just need leaders who can set the direction and craft that high-definition destination—that HDD.

What makes for a good HDD? To illustrate, consider a bombing mission and what you'd need to know. You'd need to know what target. You'd need to know where it is, how many bombs you need, what type of bombs, and what level of collateral damage you'll accept. You can't just tell a fighter pilot to just take out a target. Rest assured we will, but how will we take it out? Do we want to obliterate the entire area? Do we need a surgical strike? Is the area so heavily defended that we need a stealthy strike at night? Do our troops need to utilize the facility once the enemy is eliminated? A fighter pilot like me needs a high-definition picture of the end state so I can select my ordnance, my route, my timing, and my tactics. Vision just doesn't cut it. General ideas lead to general execution, and that gets sloppy. We have to eliminate doubt, guesswork, and ambiguity. In the military, those things kill people. A simple vision cannot adequately convey the leader's intent; it cannot provide the definition needed to enable rapid execution in a modern, complex world where no single person or team has complete knowledge. A good HDD, however, gives us the detail we need. "I want you pilots to take down that bridge so the enemy can't advance, but I want you to do it by blowing up the right side of that bridge, hitting that cement brace near the waterline so there are no civilian causalities and so I can rebuild it after the war is over and have it back in business quickly." That's pretty clear to me. That's an HDD.

A former special-forces operator and service-academy graduate left the military after a distinguished 10-year career and began managing a 50-person sales force for a medical company. He quickly discovered the company had had a problem aligning its sales teams with its corporate goals. Now, don't get me wrong. The numbers were outstanding, sales were up, and the sales teams were doing really well, particularly in smaller communities. Physicians in rural hospitals loved the company's product and were often able to make purchase decisions without involving a larger bureaucracy. The sales came easily and the numbers were great. That's where many sellers focused. What was not to like?

Turns out, plenty. Turns out, management wasn't happy. The company had a vision to see its products used in prestigious institutions like the Mayo Clinic and Johns Hopkins. Management wanted to build their product's reputation by having it used by the best physicians in the finest hospitals. But they were selling the most products in rural hospitals, facilities that wouldn't influence their targeted strategic buyers. Management wanted national leaders buying their products. They wanted the most-respected health care institutions in the nation, ones that would influence other institutions. The field sales teams were growing sales, but influential doctors weren't using the product. The sales force wasn't moving the company toward its ultimate goals. They were tactically aligned, but not organizationally aligned.

Classic misalignment. The sales team was functioning well in terms of identifying new prospects and closing sales and indeed their alignment was actually outstanding in many ways, but for all their effectiveness, they were pulling in the wrong direction. They were selling to the wrong people. The sales to small hospitals were easy and they hit their numbers and near-term revenue targets. But they weren't reaching longer-term goals that would ultimately drive more revenue. It wasn't the fault of the sales teams. Management had failed to provide a clear HDD, the sales force wasn't aligned with the leader's intent for the company, and there was a gap in strategic alignment. Leadership was going in one direction, the sales force in another.

They recognized the problem and fixed it. Leadership started to communicate a clear HDD throughout the organization and made sure it was understood in every division and department, all the way down to the sales teams. The teams developed a key account program where senior sales representatives partnered with select hospitals, shifting the focus from individual to institutional sales, particularly in urban markets. Thus, the company brought its sales force into strategic alignment and today they're closing in on that highly-defined destination.

When General Stanley McChrystal took command of the U.S. mission in Afghanistan in 2009, he knew that winning the trust of local citizens was every bit as important to America's overall goal as directly combating the Taliban. During Vietnam, many frontline leaders joked that U.S. policy was "Grab 'em by the neck and their hearts and minds will follow." That approach worked poorly for General William Westmoreland in Vietnam and General McChrystal wanted to avoid a similar outcome in his theater. In order for his policy to work, the men in the field had to understand the broader mission and act accordingly. If the privates and corporals dealing directly with Afghan citizens didn't act in support of McChrystal's vision, America would alienate the citizenry and compromise its overall mission. The general had to ensure every soldier in the chain of command understood his intent and his HDD. He wanted to defeat the Taliban, he said, but he also wanted to win the hearts and minds of the Afghans and equip them so that when U.S. forces left, citizens could rebuild their country and make it stable. In many ways, McChrystal succeeded. To illustrate a point about leader's intent, he told a story about Marine Corporal Rolando Cabezas.

Corporal Cabezas was a fire team leader operating in southwestern Afghanistan in an area where Taliban militia and improvised explosive devices (IEDs) constantly plagued coalition troops. But Taliban fighters and peaceful locals were often indistinguishable from one another. One day, a farmer approached Corporal Cabezas and explained that he needed to dig an irrigation ditch across a road, and he didn't want

U.S. soldiers to mistake him for a terrorist placing a roadside bomb. Could the marines make sure he was safe while he worked?

Seeing the potential for confusion, Corporal Cabezas dispatched his team to stand guard while the farmer dug his irrigation channel, protecting him from any troops who might misinterpret his activity. But because the corporal understood his larger responsibility, which was to win the hearts and minds of the local population, he didn't simply stand by and watch. He took off his helmet and helped the farmer dig the ditch. Throughout the day, the farmer, Corporal Cabezas, and several other U.S. Marines dug an irrigation ditch across the road. They helped the farmer cover the ditch so traffic could roll over it while water flowed beneath the road. They even reinforced it so it could bear the heaviest of loads. The farmer was so won over and grateful that he later invited those marines to a local gathering, where they celebrated the completion of the job. More than an irrigation ditch had been dug; the farmer referred to Corporal Cabezas as his son. By being aligned with his leader's intent and HDD, the corporal seized an otherwise innocuous roadside moment and turned it into a profound and personal contribution to the American mission—one that, as General McChrystal later observed, was as valuable as a millions of dollars in aid.[1]

Marine General Charles Krulak coined the phrase "strategic corporal," which perfectly describes Rolando Cabezas. In a war where soldiers need to fight, keep the peace, and render humanitarian aid, frontline leaders like corporals must have the necessary training, empowerment, and alignment to act independently in several capacities, all of which contribute to the American mission.[2] Special operations teams balance this multirole responsibility in their own way. When they arrive in foreign hotspots, they generally don't look like traditional soldiers. They want to blend in. Many have beards and

---

[1]Stanley McChrystal, "From Forward Operating Base to Boardroom," *Wall Street Journal*, May 21, 2012, A15.
[2]Charles Krulak, General, U.S. Marine Corps, "The Strategic Corporal: Leadership in the Three Block War," *Marines*, January 1999. www.au.af.mil/au/awc/awcgate/usmc/strategic_corporal.htm.

long hair. They may wear civilian clothes instead of official uniforms. Often, they speak the local language and know the customs. They are highly trained warriors, but they are also ambassadors and diplomats. Their missions frequently involve working collaboratively with locals and even providing them direct assistance. It can be tough to do that with guns and grenades on your hip.

So, look at your own company. Are your frontline troops aligned with your strategy? Do they understand your HDD; do they trust it; can they envision it? Can they act independently to help achieve your intent? The downside can be disastrous, particularly in the age of viral videos and social media. Hewlett-Packard (HP) got snowed with negative publicity in 2008 over a botched laptop repair. The company, which strives to be known for its customer service, received a laptop with a malfunctioning hinge. The device was still under warranty. When the technician opened the laptop, liquid spilled onto his own computer, damaging his motherboard. The computer's owner received a bill for $1,099 to fix the technician's motherboard. The story went viral and HP wisely retreated, but not before tech blogs had assailed the company's reputation. Because the frontline customer service and technical personnel weren't empowered to act in the customer's best interest, they weren't in alignment with HP's aim to have great service. The company received a wave of negative publicity, and that one black eye made the public forget about thousands of other instances of great service.[3]

A similar incident happened at Delta Airlines. Per standard policy, an airline agent charged a unit of soldiers returning from Afghanistan $200 each to check a fourth piece of luggage; the unit's bill tallied $2,800. Of course, the tired soldiers protested, but the agent was inflexible. On the flight back home, the soldiers recorded a video expressing their displeasure at Delta's unfriendly welcome after their long deployment to Afghanistan. The video hit the Internet and went

---

[3]Devin Coldewey, "HP Attempts to Charge Customer $1099 Due to 'Liquid Inside Keyboard,'" July 4, 2008. http://techcrunch.com/2008/07/04/hp-attempts-to-charge-customer-1099-due-to-liquid-inside-keyboard/.

viral to Delta's detriment. I have no doubt that Delta's leaders never intended for something like that to happen, but who communicated that to the desk agent? Apparently no one. Shortly thereafter, Delta changed its policy to allow troops returning from deployment to check a fourth bag at no charge. Had their frontline customer service representative had greater discretion, the negative publicity might have been avoided.[4]

The point is, the world is changing and news spreads fast, so it's doubly important for your people to understand your long-term HDD *and* have the power to make those fine adjustments on the spot so they can help you achieve it. How many other instances do you know of where employees make blatantly poor decisions because they follow written procedures instead of their leaders' real intent? Good companies clearly communicate their HDD and empower their people to help them achieve it.

On the positive side, Xerox did an outstanding job of this. They developed a standard question to ask customers after each interaction: "Given the situation you faced and the action we have taken to respond, are you now more or less loyal to Xerox?" Every customer-facing employee knew about the question—and understood their role in getting the customer to answer, "More." Everyone understood management's HDD and they were empowered to take actions to move the company toward that destination. They began employing that strategic question in 2011. By year-end, net revenue had jumped 32 percent.

When leaders know their troops are well trained and understand the broader mission, they have peace of mind; they have faith that their troops can take the steps needed to achieve the unit's goals. When their units encounter problems, which they inevitably will, these leaders can trust their chain of command to do the right thing.

In combat and business, individual execution is one thing; organizational execution is everything. Today's environment demands that the

---

[4]Joan Lowy and Joshua Freed, "Delta Bag Fees for Soldiers Ignites Backlash," *Army Times*, June 6, 2011. www.armytimes.com/article/20110608/NEWS/106080304/Delta-bag-fees-soldiers-ignites-backlash.

entire organization works together, in alignment, to survive, thrive, and ultimately dominate. And that comes back to the HDD. The organization needs a clear, compelling, and high-definition picture of its destination. Troops need a detailed image of where they're heading so they can all work together toward that destination and keep things on track when problems arise.

For an illustration, just look at an aircraft carrier. Corporal Cabezas and his fellow troops in Afghanistan could count on air support from U.S. carriers stationed off the coast of Pakistan. Carrier strike groups, with their thousands of men, destroyers, frigates, and centerpiece floating airport, are impressive but when I look at that carrier strike group, I don't see the ships, jets, or teams of people. I see two things: *alignment* and *leader's intent*. The men and women on the flight deck and in the engine room aren't executing based on what they *think* the captain wants, they're working from a high-definition destination picture of *exactly* what the captain wants—which in this case, is to keep the carrier deck launching and recovering jets.

"There's an awful lot going on out there—thousands of pieces," said Dee Mewbourne, commanding officer of the USS *Eisenhower*, as he looked over his carrier's flight deck. Below him, men were scrambling with equipment and hoses, planes were landing and taxiing, and bombs were being carted across the deck. At regular intervals, a jet took off on a mission into Afghanistan. "If you had to launch one airplane and you had to go through a step-by-step checklist—what it required from staring up the reactors to loading up food to getting flight physicals to getting the jet topside and ready—if you have to list it all, it'd be a million steps or more. I can't worry about every little thing."

"To make it happen, we have to empower people to do their individual jobs. We give them the tools they need—things like priorities, tasks, and authority. Then we get all our people pulling together and those launches seem to happen effortlessly every 45 seconds. It's amazing."

Actually, it's not amazing. It's a process. It's clearly communicating the leader's intent. A good HDD inspires personal performance *and* ingenuity. The men and women aboard *Eisenhower* shared a single high-definition destination for the American mission in Afghanistan. Since carriers operate more in the tactical realm, they translated that HDD into specific strategies and mission objectives. They aimed to be a flawlessly executing airbase that supported the U.S. mission in Afghanistan. That meant their flight deck had to be safe, their cata-pults had to function, their aircraft had to take off and land, and their arresting gear needed to be working. They were aligning with the captain's intent. That HDD cascaded through every level and every department of the carrier, becoming specific and measurable mission objectives for every team and individual on the ship.

Interestingly, Captain Mewbourne had to use a separate and largely internal HDD to preserve the remarkable level of excellence on his own ship. When he became the captain of *Eisenhower*, he inherited a ship that already exhibited exceptionally high performance and high morale, which worried him. He feared the ship would fall prey to the cycle of natural atrophy that leads to a decline in performance and mishaps. How could he combat that? How could he keep his ship functioning at such a high level over an extended period, like a six-month deployment?

He kept his team focused on the HDD established by America's regional commanders, but he also inspired them with a new vision: "Greater each day." Typically, that statement might be too vague to drive precise effects, but Captain Mewbourne empowered his subor-dinates to make that vision crystal clear and to have it repeated for their individual departments and teams. He empowered his department heads and other lower-echelon leaders to create small-scale HDDs for their departments, to create images of their ideal destinations. When they reached that HDD, they'd have to devise an even loftier one. Hoping to maintain the ship's level of high performance, department leaders encouraged their men and women to improve in some way every day and to ask themselves, "How can I do better?"

When *Eisenhower's* number three arresting gear assembly broke dur-ing flight operations, Captain Mewbourne didn't spend time devising a solution or overseeing repairs. The men and women responsible already knew their mission objective was ensuring four wires were operational; that was part of the HDD for the carrier deck and it was a small part of the overall HDD of providing combat air support inland. To realize the HDD, they had to fix the three-wire. They had contingency plans for a malfunction, which they had practiced so when the real problem occurred, they were able to fix it quickly so full operations could continue. Their training taught them how to make the repair and they did their job. Their department was aligned with the ship's larger mission. How did they achieve that alignment? Captain Mewbourne and other leaders communicated a clear, high-definition destination (HDD), and a compelling vision. Then, they cascaded it through every department, right down to the deckplates. They empowered leaders throughout the ship.

THE BUILDING BLOCKS

For people to act like Corporal Cabezas or the *Eisenhower's* crew, General McChrystal had to put high definition around the future he wanted for Afghanistan. That detailed concept enabled all his troops to act better, target better, and deploy processes more effectively. You need this in business, too. Your teams need the same understanding that an aircraft carrier's crew has of their common destination, expressed in that same, detailed, high definition. But how do you accomplish that? Building a high-definition destination comes from drilling down in five key areas. Consider it an inventory assessment and a self-examination at the same time.

1. **Human**. Consider your organization's future culture, workforce, benefits, and compensation, then, think about how you'll motivate, train, and engage your employees to ensure they're aligned with your corporate mission.
2. **Market**. Determine in which product/service and geographic markets you'll compete, and define what your brand will represent. What industries will you serve and how will you work with and relate to the public?

3. **Financial**. What does financial success look like at your destination? What goals will let you know you've arrived?
4. **Structural**. Decide how your organization will be structured and incorporated in the future. Define the assets you expect to have (e.g., real estate, buildings, equipment, infrastructure, etc.).
5. **Entrepreneurship**. Will you be an innovator or a quick-reactor to others? What type of research and development process will you have? What types of risks are you willing to take?

All these related questions help answer your one big question: "Where are we going?" That end state is your high-definition destination. Remember, it's not one specific goal. Rather, it's a clear description of what your organization will look like when it arrives at its future destination: What will success look like in three years? In five? For sales, for production, for HR, for investors? The HDD must contain details that can provide measurable goals for teams and employees such that they ensure the organization can align itself, top to bottom.

A good HDD can be replicated at every level of an organization. Each relevant business unit or department should create that high-definition destination for their area. The HDD for one department may differ from another, but they will both align with the organization's overall intended destination. As a fighter pilot, I understood the HDD envisioned by the air force for our global mission and the HDD set forth by my fighter wing—and I knew exactly how I needed to act to reach both of those destinations.

But nothing happens if things aren't measured, so it's vital for groups to determine what specific metrics will gauge their progress. Assigning measures begins to set the idea of accountability and someone, *one person*, should ultimately own responsibility for each measure. Personal accountability is essential. We measure tactics in business with countless methods, but rarely do we challenge our business to measure the progress to our most important thing: our high-definition destination, our HDD!

Seasoned executive Dan McAtee took over leadership of a major international steel company, with operations in 35 countries, including England, Pakistan, Colombia, and Vietnam. His challenge was to align these disparate and diverse groups of facilities and employees behind common goals. Instead of turning to major consulting firms or complicated methodologies, he chose to combat complexity with simplicity. He gathered stakeholders from across the organization, from an array of countries, functional areas, and levels, and worked with them to develop a common high-definition destination. Over two days, they created an HDD that the group collectively and individually owned. What did the future look like for the organization as a whole? What did it look like for individual business units and departments? What measurements would track progress and how would they hold everyone accountable? They had all the answers and they all agreed to hold themselves and each other accountable for progress.

But it wasn't a perfect plan. McAtee called it a 75 percent plan, but that was enough. He explained, "Working with other methodologies, I've spent too much time trying to get perfect data. You just can't do it or do it expediently. And I'm a Six Sigma black belt! So we all came up with a simple plan together. It was a 75 percent solution, but that was important. It got us moving together in a common direction, being accountable to one another. And the process builds in feedback and adjustment, so we'll figure out the remaining 25 percent as we go. The important thing is that we're moving forward together. We have a bias for action."[5]

Alignment and common purpose helped the company in numerous areas, including their philanthropy. Prior to the team's alignment around the new HDD, the charitable giving steering committee had long processes and often long debates that determined what organizations received grants. During the organization planning exercise, the team decided to focus corporate giving on areas that would help the community where they operated while building the corporate brand. Since they manufactured nails and wire, they targeted construction-related charities like Habitat for Humanity.

---

[5]Dan McAtee. Interview with the author, August 11, 2013.

"The new process was a win–win," McAtee said. "We started allocating limited resources in an effective way and avoiding fights! Our alignment vastly improved the decision-making process because we could test options against our agreed-upon HDD. If the charity wasn't aligned, it made our decision easy." Across the company, employees at all levels could test initiatives against the company's defined objectives. Did they fit or not? A shared mental model drove everyone's decision-making process regarding products, new hires, or businesses in which the company would or would not invest. There were no complicated formulas, just empowered employees who bought into a common HDD and agreed to hold each other accountable.

The real test came, though, when the financial markets melted down in 2008. "When the financial crisis came, this process kept the company above water," McAtee said. "Our demand dropped by 20 percent, but we still grew at 5 percent, even in that environment. Our people could execute against our plan and make needed adjustments locally since they were empowered and understood the HDD."[6]

Sometimes organization *itself* makes the critical difference. When candidates enter BUD/S, the SEAL training program, they learn very quickly to become team members, not individuals. They do everything as small groups, often called pods. Aspiring SEALs learn very quickly that the most important people are the ones on their team. In training in San Diego, these special operators thrive and execute within their pods.

Those concepts weren't lost on 2008 U.S. Ryder Cup team captain Paul Azinger. The United States had dropped three matches in a row to the European team; they hadn't yet won in the twenty-first century. Azinger felt tremendous pressure to win back the trophy, and he had a crystal clear picture of his desired destination: 12 American golfers gathered around a golden trophy, smiling broadly, arm-in-arm because they had won as a team. So he took an unorthodox approach, at least for professional golf. He knew about the SEALs' focus on small teams and thought the approach could work for him. He believed the pods

---

[6] Ibid.

approach could meld highly-competitive golfers like Phil Mickelson, Stewart Cink, and Jim Furyk into a cohesive team that could win the Ryder Cup. It would be a radical departure from any strategy previously employed in the tournament's 82-year history, but the traditional methods hadn't worked for the Americans in almost 10 years so why not? Maybe, Azinger thought, this new system would have players that traditionally competed against each other suddenly pulling for one another.

"Tour players are hardwired to beat the guys next to them," Azinger explained, "Then one week [every two years] we think they should go against their nature and become a championship team. But maybe 12 is too big. If you want to bring the Ryder Cup team together, maybe you have to break it apart." Just like the SEALs.[7]

When time arrived for Azinger to select his team, he didn't simply pick 12 pros. In fact, he didn't even pick all the team members. Six players had made the team by virtue of PGA Ryder Cup standings, and Azinger sorted them into three groups of two that would act as their SEAL pods, their boat crews. Azinger considered how other golfers would mesh with each two-man team and he picked the third member of each pod accordingly. He studied the three three-man pods and assessed their character, personalities, strengths, and weaknesses. Based on that, he culled a list of players who might fit well with each group, and gave the list to each pod. Azinger then empowered the three-man pods to pick their own fourth member from his list of options. It was Phil Mickelson, Anthony Kim, and Justin Leonard who chose Hunter Mahan. Jim Furyk, Kenny Perry, and Boo Weekley chose J. B. Holmes. Stewart Cink, Ben Curtis, and Steve Stricker chose Chad Campbell. Thus, Azinger's 2008 Ryder Cup team came together as three separate teams of four similar personalities. He'd designed the pods so genuine friendship and mutual support could develop among traditional rivals. He hoped it would work.

---

[7]Paul Azinger, *Cracking the Code: The Winning Ryder Cup Strategy: Make It Work for You* (Decatur, GA: Looking Glass Books, 2010), Kindle edition.

At Valhalla Golf Club in Louisville, Kentucky, the U.S. team spent more time in their pods than with the full team. In fact, the players rarely spent any time with players *not* in their pods. Each golfer focused on the three others and tight bonds developed quickly. They practiced together, ate together, and were paired together for matches.

"We played together, won together, and lost together," explained Ryder Cup veteran Stewart Cink. "We leaned on each other for support. It doesn't always go your way and your confidence can take a hit, but I had the guys in the pod to support me and they knew I was there to do the same for them."

In contrast, Nick Faldo's European team seemed less organized and cohesive, appearing haphazardly at the course for practice. Maybe they were overconfident; after all, the United States hadn't won since 1999. Sure enough, when the dust settled on Sunday afternoon, the American team had reclaimed the Ryder Cup.

"We got the win and I really think it was because Zinger divided us into pods," explained Cink. "It made our task seem manageable. My task was helping guys in my pod play well and win points. If we did that, I knew we'd do our part for the larger team. The other pods felt the same way. When we added it up, we had the points to win. If you're part of a team of 12, it can feel overwhelming. It's hard to explain, but it just seemed more manageable in pods."[8]

Simplicity combats complexity.

Remember, individual execution is one thing, but organizational execution is everything. In BUD/S, nobody measures you on your own ability. You're measured by how well your team performs. Likewise, a victorious team, not a single golfer, hoists the Ryder Cup. European team member Padraig Harrington had won two majors that year, the Open Championship and the PGA Championship, but that didn't matter. The American *team* won. Team members need that base of core skills, but if they're not aligned as a team, good execution just can't happen.

---

[8]Stewart Cink. Interview with the author, August 19, 2013.

DEVELOPING LEADERS

Alignment. What a powerful word. And such an elusive concept. Many business or organizations have superstars, but can they achieve organizational success alone? Doubtful. It takes an entire organization aligned behind a clearly-communicated and highly-defined future destination.

Once soldiers and sailors finish their initial military training and indoc, they're capable individuals with the foundation and potential to execute missions on a high-performing combat team—but first they must get aligned. The alignment phase of development forges them into team members. For navy SEALs, this comes during the first phase of their training program. They've received their basic training and most have served time in the fleet; now, they're trying to become special operators and they quickly learn that there are no lone wolves among the SEALs. You become a team player or you don't make it.

Naval Academy graduate Mark McGinnis never planned to become a Navy SEAL, but not long after graduation, he found himself reporting to Naval Amphibious Base Coronado, just outside San Diego, California. Coronado hosts the navy's West Coast SEAL teams and serves as the proving ground for aspiring elite sailors and officers.

"You make the leap from individuals to team member in first phase BUD/S," McGinnis explained. "You figure out very quickly that you're not going to make it by yourself. If you don't become a team player and care about peers more than yourself, you'll wash out. We don't have mavericks."

Many civilians think of SEALs as loners, but that's a misconception. If SEAL candidates don't have a team orientation in their first week, they'll surely have it by the second week. SEALs work and operate as teams and every competition in training is a team competition. There are no individual prizes; crews either work together or lose. And believe me, they don't want to lose. If teammates are struggling, others must help them however they can. Sometimes, a team member will drop back and verbally encourage a lagging buddy; at other times they'll half-carry him. If a team finishes last on a run, everyone gets punished, not just the slowest runner. Punishment means join-ing the goon squad for push-ups, getting wet and sandy in the chilly Pacific surf, running, or other unpleasantries. The SEAL candidates must become a team quickly, or wash out trying. When new SEALs receive their trident pin and assignment to one of the active SEAL teams, they understand how to function as a group of professionals. "We expect to lead and be led," says the SEAL ethos. "In the absence of orders I will take charge, lead my teammates and accomplish the mission." *Teammates.*

The value of teamwork is the hallmark of success in almost every organized human endeavor. Teams create alignment, which adds mutual support. But even with teams, only 17 out of 244 men who started the class with McGinnis earned their pins on time. The six-month gauntlet is that tough.

Which turns our attention to tactics. With its individual warriors forged into teams, elite units are ready for their mission. Troops at all levels share a common mindset and organizational identity. They're aligned behind a common HDD. They have the confidence and knowledge to plan and eventually execute strategies and actions that will help their organization reach its intended destination.

Now it's time for tactics.

MISSION CHECKLIST

Aligned Teams:
1. Create and pursue a common high definition destination.
2. Maintain situational awareness at all times.
3. Utilize cross checks to monitor threats and progress toward goals.
4. Communicate the leader's intent to all organizational levels.
5. Empower frontline troops or employees via a clear HDD.

CHAPTER 4

MISSION PREPARATION: MOVING FROM STRATEGY TOWARD ACCOUNTABLE ACTIONS

American strategists planning 1991's Operation Desert Storm undertook one of the largest, most complex planning challenges in recent U.S. military history. Their job was aligning soldiers, ships, aircraft, missiles, equipment, and supporting resources from 32 countries to achieve the goal of expelling Saddam Hussein's troops from Kuwait. Coalition leaders relied on a doctrine known as effects-based operations (EBO). Proponents argued that by identifying and bombing a limited number of strategic targets, you could achieve the precise effect you want. So what effect do you want?

In 1991, the coalition's ultimate goal was to get the Iraqi army out of Kuwait with a minimum loss of civilian life. To achieve that intended effect, planners blueprinted the country of Iraq. They mapped out the interrelated connections that made up the power grids, communication networks, roads and airports, and military command-and-control networks. Then they set out to identify the key nodes, the centers of gravity, the leverage points. Essentially they asked themselves, "Where would a precision bomb do the most overall damage? The loss of which asset would cause the biggest network disruption and give us the most bang for our buck?" Planners identified the power grid. Electricity powered the country's command and control facilities so planners worked backwards from a desired end state: an Iraq without electrical power. How could they best achieve that effect?

First objective: Turn out the lights in Baghdad in the first five minutes of battle. Second objective: Shut down electricity throughout Iraq in 24 hours. Planners also had an overriding condition: Minimize civilian casualties.

Three major electrical plants powered Iraq and attacking those would quickly blackout most every house, street, and military base in the country, but destroying them would also entail significant loss of life and make rebuilding the country difficult and costly. So instead, planners identified a small number of voltage regulators as their critical leverage points. Attacking those leverage points would affect the entire system while causing very few casualties, since most were in rural areas, although significant repairs would still be necessary to bring the system back online after the bombing.

The generals in charge staged a planning conference and included field commanders and their staffs; top echelon leaders would benefit from in-the-field perspective and knowledge. As they narrowed the target list and began making decisions about which aircraft and weapons to employ, one lower-ranking officer brought up a newly-developed weapon that could shut down electrical transformers without causing permanent damage. When American F-117 stealth fighters slipped into Iraq in January 1991, they carried bombs containing aluminum chaff, which performed as promised, shorting out the voltage regulators and causing minimal damage and casualties in the process. The lights went out and the Americans liberated Kuwait and avoided civilian casualties.

That's effects-based targeting.

That's the power of leverage points. What are they in your world?

CRITICAL LEVERAGE POINTS

In any combat environment, victory goes to the force that can identify and control the right pressure points. This isn't a recent development. Look at the story of David and Goliath. David knew where to target his slingshot for maximum effect: between the giant's eyes. Every person, every army, every system has vulnerabilities. To win, you have to identify them and apply the right pressure, be it a slingshot, a bomb, or a blockade. In the American Civil War, General William Sherman recognized the value of capturing the railroad hub of Atlanta. The capture of Atlanta effectively choked the South's last internal supply lines; the Union blockade of the Southern ports had effectively closed off international trade. The war ended nine months after Atlanta fell. Even 150 years ago, military planners leveraged pressure points.

Unfortunately, the enemy also knows about critical leverage points, and often builds in hidden contingency plans. In World War II, Allied bombers attacked Germany's industrial centers, aiming to destroy the Axis's ability to wage war. In particular, they targeted the German aircraft industry. Their aircraft factories and component makers were spread all across the country; the original Allied target list had more than 300 locations. Disabling them all could take years. On the other hand, every aircraft needed an engine and every engine needed ball bearings, so if the Allies could just shut down the German ball bearing plants, they could halt the production of engines—which would halt the production of new German fighters. Conveniently, nearly all of the German ball bearing factories were clustered in and around the city of Schweinfurt. On August 17, 1942, the Allies sent more than 350 B-17 bombers in to destroy the factories. Sixty bombers were lost; nearly 100 were badly damaged, but the factories were hit hard. Still, the production of German aircraft continued. The Germans made *steel* ball bearings at Schweinfurt, but they made millions of synthetic ones at other plants, and two neutral countries sold Germany supplies. The raids did little good.

The Allies were still convinced of the value of attacking leverage points, so they tried again. Planners turned their attention to the German oil network. By bombing a relatively small number of refineries, the Allies were finally able to cripple a network by attacking key nodes. Using bombs against a small number of key targets, they turned off the flow of gasoline to the German Luftwaffe and both fighter planes and Panzer tanks ran out of gas.

BUSINESS LEVERAGE POINTS

The late 1990s saw the beginning of the digital revolution. Where before one had to buy a bulky cassette or CD player to enjoy music on the go, content suddenly went digital. With just a few clicks, music could now be downloaded onto your computer and burned to all sorts of media that in turn could be played by all sorts of devices. The Sony Walkman and Discman, which played tapes and CDs, was fast replaced by a clever little thing called an iPod, which was digital.

That's how it ended up. But how did it get there? Well, it started out on the wrong foot and it seemed like the digital revolution was going to be dead before it got going. Digital copies of songs were being illegally shared on the Internet. Record companies and artists saw revenue losses, lawyers got into action to protect copyrights, the revolution looked like a swamp. Several companies, including Microsoft and HP, tried to capitalize on the new model, but failed. Behind the headlines, Apple had its head down and was hard at work trying to figure out the new ecosystem. "What do we have to do to make money from this disruption?" they asked. Smart people. While others were panicking and suing and trying to *stop* the spread of digital music, Apple was trying to fix it, harness it, and accelerate it. The secret, they believed, would unfold only if they mapped out the entire music industry and found the leverage points the way military planners blueprinted Iraq's entire infrastructure. Sure enough, they found seven critical leverage points that if addressed properly would lead to a breakthrough, a revolution in itself.

1. **A device**. Apple was the first to admit that playback devices were clunky. If millions of 18-year-olds were going to carry something, it had to have a big cool factor. Apple knew cool factors. They put their designers to work.

2. **Earphones**. One of the first barriers to acceptance of portable music players was their oafish, low-fidelity headphones. That would have to change and it did. Apple developed compact, user-friendly, high-fidelity earphones that were light and breezy. Then Apple smartly made commercials showing the earphones as an accessory to a footloose lifestyle.

3. **A source for music downloads (iTunes)**. Apple had to set people's mind at ease and show artists and record companies a way to sell music downloads without enabling illegal sharing. Apple created a technology platform that could download music, get it on a user's device, protect the copyright, and ensure the accounting was handled properly, sending royalties and payments to all parties. And they gave the software away for free.

4. **Artists**. Artists and royalty owners had to see that Apple could sell their music and protect their royalties. Apple realized that by convincing the right celebrity artists that their system worked and that it protected their music while also generating millions in new revenues for them, well, others would fall in line. Apple

lined up some of the biggest names in music behind iTunes: U2 and Lenny Kravitz. The rest is history.

5. **Record companies**. Same problem with the record companies. Apple needed to convince them that iTunes could control pirating and generate revenues. Sony Records signed on, giving Apple an invaluable—and mutually profitable—relationship with a traditional music powerhouse. In months, nearly every other record company had joined in.

6. **Trend-setters**. One gets a disproportionate return by engaging trend-setters, so Apple chose to focus their sales pitch on university students, knowing that if college students used Apple's devices and software, younger teens would adopt it, as would post-college young adults. They found and targeted the right customers.

7. **Price**. Finally, the device had to be affordable and the downloads had to be as inexpensive as possible. When iTunes launched, downloads were offered at 99 cents, below the $1 barrier. The company set the price point for the iPod devices at under $350 and ensured the new product was ready for Christmas in 2001.

We know the rest of that story. Leverage points. Centers of gravity. Action. Today, Apple still owns the lion's share of the digital music market—their first-mover's premium. Pioneering the iPod drove Apple on toward more innovation. It transformed itself from a static computer company into one of the world's most dynamic and successful providers of entertainment, knowledge, connectivity, and experiences.

LEVELS OF PLANNING

Every year, businesses across the nation plan. They forecast sales, announce goals, and commit resources to hitting targets, but as the months march by, their plans fall off track. By the year's end, the company hasn't reached its goal. We call that an *execution gap*, the difference between where you planned to be and where you wound up. Companies often fall short during execution because their tactics don't align with their overall strategy. As we said earlier, American business has an execution problem.

For example, a sales department can be selling a tremendous volume of product to a client with deep pockets and high demand, but what if they're selling a low-margin product, or one that's not aligned with the company's intended direction? You can be tactically excellent, but never reach your goals if your actions aren't aligned with your envisioned high-definition destination.

Once leadership casts its HDD and aligns its people and teams with the overall goal, it's time to begin executing missions and progressing toward that intended destination. Before air force teams embark on a mission, we enter into an extensive and highly structured planning process that ensures we have the necessary resources and preparation to achieve the mission objective. The old adage "fail to plan, plan to fail" certainly applies.

The air force conducts planning on three levels, what I call organizational, strategic, and tactical. As our people go through the planning process, we ensure their plans are aligned with one another and, ultimately, with the air force HDD, which has already been set in the high-level organizational planning process. That's where we make an overall plan that covers a three-to-five-year period.

After that, we have the strategic plans and the tactical plans. Multiple strategic plans will support an overarching organizational plan, while multiple tactical plans will support a strategic plan. The strategic level is where we're targeting the systems and leverage points we need to affect in order to reach our desired HDD. Think of history's great military campaigns: Yorktown, Gettysburg, Midway, Normandy. Each of these initiatives supported the larger objective of wining wars—the American Revolution, the Civil War, and World War II. They were large operations that targeted critical leverage points that would, hopefully, help break the enemy. George Washington defeated General Charles Cornwallis's British army at Yorktown, Virginia, to end the Revolutionary War. Union general George Meade struck a mortal blow to Confederate General Robert E. Lee's Army of Northern Virginia at Gettysburg, Pennsylvania, to turn the tide of the

Civil War. During World War II, key battles were fought at Midway Island and on the beaches of Normandy. At Midway, the Americans sank the Japanese carriers that protected their vital Pacific network, while D-Day opened a second front on the increasingly-stretched German army. None of those campaigns alone won their respective wars outright; rather they were important strategic steps, each with multiple attacks, raids, and missions supporting the overall goals and strategic plan.

Organizational plans focus on winning wars. Strategic plans win campaigns and battles. The strategic level of planning focuses on actions with time horizons of 12, 18, or 24 months. Each leverage point you decide to attack needs a strategic plan that coordinates the resources you'll bring to bear. Each strategic plan therefore needs to be broken down into the smaller plans—what jets, what bombs, what targets, how much fuel. Those are tactical plans.

How do you support a strategic plan, like the one supporting Operation Overlord (D-Day)? With tactical plans. And therein lies the real action.

THE FLAWLESS EXECUTION ENGINE: *PLAN, BRIEF, EXECUTE, DEBRIEF*

Colonel John Boyd flew air force fighters during the Korean and Vietnam wars and began making observations about how one aircraft could gain advantage over another. He realized the pilot who could most quickly assess a situation and act would fly home after the dogfight; the other pilot would get shot down. In aerial combat, a pilot has to constantly assess his position relative to the ground and to his adversary, then maneuver accordingly. The better the pilot, the more rapidly he could complete this cycle of assessment and reaction. Eventually, Boyd named the cycle the OODA loop for observe, orient, decide, act. He was thinking cyclically, not linearly, and realized the winning pilot got *inside* the decision cycle of their adversary. They could cycle through the OODA loop more quickly. The victors could react faster and better. That's how they seized the critical advantage.

Battlefields and global commerce have grown more complex and teams have become central to the function of armored divisions and commercial firms alike. To adjust, we converted the OODA loop from an individual tool to a group tool that's critically important to each level of planning. Let's look at the tactical level. Once organizational planning has yielded a long-term HDD and identified critical leverage points over a three-to-five-year span, and once strategic planning has developed plans with 12-to-24-month horizons to affect each critical leverage point, tactically-focused teams begin planning the individual missions that must be accomplished. These battlefield-level actions will affect leverage points, impact the entire targeted system, and thus achieve the organization's HDD. Time horizons here are typically short, from a few hours out to 30, 60, or 90 days. This is tactical execution, this is our bread and butter. This is what elite U.S. military teams do better than anyone else in the world, even in the most complex and hostile environments. Here's the reason: We combat complexity with simplicity.

Using our experience with high-performing military units and with high-performing businesses, our company distilled that idea of simplicity into a four-step cycle: *plan, brief, execute, and debrief.* Those four steps are our key to disciplined tactical execution in any organization and any level. It's the evolution of the OODA loop, and it includes that all-important last component, *debriefing*, which allows us to adjust rapidly to constant change. We get better each cycle.

At Afterburner, we call his four-step loop the Flawless Execution cycle: *plan, brief, execute, debrief.* It's not just a cycle; it's an engine that empowers high-performance teams. *Plan, brief, execute, debrief.* We plan every mission, then brief the mission to the men and women we'll hold accountable to carry it out. After we brief, we go out and execute. When the mission ends, we don't immediately go plan again. Instead, we go to a room and debrief in a nameless, rankless environment. For the moment, we set aside our positions or ranks; they don't matter. We freely admit our errors and successes in front of peers, supervisors, and subordinates. It's *what's* right, not *who's* right. We get the lessons on the table so nobody on the team will repeat our mistakes, and we aim to repeat the high points. We walk away with lessons learned and put them back into the next planning cycle. Doing that demands a rankless environment where everyone can contribute on even footing, for the good of the whole.

The Flawless Execution cycle repeats most rapidly at the tactical level, where planning horizons can be hours or days. The framework applies at the strategic and organizational levels of planning as well, although at those levels, the cycle time will be longer. You may not be holding debriefs every week, but rather quarterly or yearly. Whatever your time horizon for planning, if you follow the disciplined cycle of planning, briefing, executing, and debriefing, you'll achieve your intended effect on your key leverage points and reach your HDD. And in the process, you'll be moving at or ahead of the rate of change, even in a complex marketplace or hostile battlespace.

ELEMENTS OF SUCCESSFUL PLANNING

Successful plans for anything, introducing a new product or winning a battlefield campaign, share several key elements. Fundamentally, good plans include a process for problem solving and have a clear, envisioned goal. Good plans will be adaptable, iterative, based on experience. They'll have well-defined courses of action, rely on realistic resources, and include an accurate risk assessment.

Since the military does almost everything with teams, its plans have certain specific elements that help get the most from team performance. High-risk military operations rely on the judgment of elite professionals in rapidly-changing combat situations, so plans are naturally decentralized. The secretary of defense cannot anticipate what conditions or surprises might affect a brigade in Afghanistan six months out. At all levels, good plans empower unit leaders close to the action to make decisions that will accomplish their missions and support a clearly defined HDD.

No team of Army Green Berets has ever gone into combat by itself. And if just Green Berets conducted mission planning, they'd barely get off the ground. Even covert military operations call upon diverse resources. Men must be transported to marshaling points; they'll need to coordinate with the 160th Special Operations Aviation Regiment, the Night Stalkers, who specialize in inserting and extracting special operations troops. They'll need to coordinate with regular army divisions to ensure they have food, shelter, equipment, and ammunition at their marshaling point and for the mission itself. They might need support on the ground, so the spec ops team will bring personnel from artillery and air support groups into the planning process. Military plans are exceedingly diverse and involve representatives from numerous divisions, squadrons, and other units. In today's world, army, air force, navy, and marine elements may plan joint missions, necessitating representatives from different branches to be present for planning sessions.

But for all the complexity of different units and phases, military planners strive to shave down a plan to its essence. The simpler the better. The more complex, the more likely something will go wrong, the more likely you'll lose focus or make a mistake. A simple plan also tends to support initiative on the part of those closer to the battle. It will empower them to act according to the situation they observe. If a plan calls for too many levels of confirmation for a decision, someone could be dead or an opportunity lost forever before the unit on-scene gets permission to act. Good plans empower people who understand the mission objective and the HDD. Finally, military planning relies on accountability, and nothing is more important to good execution. Every element of a plan needs someone's name attached to it. Let me repeat: *Someone* must be responsible, otherwise execution suffers. Simply put, tasks with names assigned tend to get accomplished.

To design simple plans that are decentralized, developed with a diverse team, support initiative, and hold individuals accountable, the military uses a careful process. We've taken that military DNA and created a defined six-step planning process that works in the civilian world. Following these steps has led to effectively executed military and business missions all around the world. Yes, they're simple, but that's exactly why they have proven so effective at all levels. Simplicity combats complexity.

Six Steps of Effective Planning
1. Determine the mission objective.
2. Identify the threats.
3. Identify available and necessary resources.
4. Evaluate lessons learned.
5. Develop a course of action (COA).
6. Plan for contingencies.

Determine the Mission Objective

Good objectives should be clear, measurable, achievable, and support the high-definition destination. The military always uses simple, easily understandable language and so should you.

- **Measurable**. You'll need specific measures so you can gauge your progress and know when your mission is accomplished. Measures are also needed for the mission debrief. Remember: If you can't measure it, it won't happen.
- **Achievable**. In a world where plans can put lives on the line, you better make sure your plans are believable and achievable. Don't set an unreasonably difficult objective, one that sets your team up for failure. Challenging? Great; they'll put their hearts into it. Nearly impossible? No; you'll lose them.
- **Aligned with the HDD**. Motivated teams understand how their mission and their tasks will help achieve the organization's over-arching goals. Ensure your plans clearly support strategy and that you teams support your plans.

Identify the Threats

What can adversely affect your mission? What knowns or unknowns are you aware of that can derail your team as you move toward your goals? How can you manage the threats out there, be they internal or external?

- **External threats**. What legal requirements, economic shifts, or environmental factors could impact our mission?

- **Internal threats**. Are budget cuts a threat? Will leadership support the plan? Do we have the necessary expertise?
- **Controllable or uncontrollable**. Can we negate, mitigate, or avoid the threats, and if so, how?

When planning, remember that threats aren't global—at least not the ones with which you're concerned. You're worried about threats that are aligned with a clear, measurable mission objective—what specific threats stand between you and your specified goals? As you categorize them as controllable or uncontrollable, be careful. Entirely uncontrollable threats are less common; there's usually a way to control a threat to some degree. We deal with these uncontrollable threats in a separate step: step six. We can't afford to have anything derail our mission or compromise our objective. You may not be able to prevent the threat from arising, but you can certainly take smart steps to manage it if it does.

Identify Available and Necessary Resources

There's not a battlefield commander out there who couldn't achieve his objective if he or she had access to unlimited resources: skilled troops, the best air support, legions of tanks, and anything else they'd need. High-performing military teams have to plan in reality, however. We should consider our objective and make our plan in the context of the available resources. Sometimes we're fortunate and we can tap a range of assets. Other times, leaders must plan and execute missions with the bare minimum. Sometimes they embark on a mission relying more on their unit's ability to execute than on their equipment or backup resources. Whatever your project, consider your resources across several categories:

- **Physical**. Do you have the necessary infrastructure?
- **Training**. What preparation and skills will your team need to achieve its goals, and where will they find them?
- **Leadership**. Who can serve as advocates at higher (or lower) levels to help mitigate internal threats, champion your plan, and secure resources?

- **People**. What skill sets, departments, and specific individuals can help you develop your plan and reach your goals?
- **External clients and customers**. How can you leverage your broader network to achieve your goals?
- **Fiscal resources**. Do you have access to adequate funds?
- **Technologies**. While being aware of fiscal constraints, leverage technology—new technology in particular—to the extent possible.
- **Known strengths**. Finally, rely on your team's talents and core competencies. Teams can get distracted and forget what they're best at doing. Don't let that happen! Your best asset is often your best skill or trait.

Sum up your research by asking, "Can our resources help us negate, mitigate, or avoid our above listed threats?"

Evaluate Lessons Learned

Tap colleagues in your organization or other resources to learn about results of similar projects. Organizations and individuals waste prodigious amounts of time reinventing the wheel or trying to implement a solution that has failed before. Generally, the same approach yields the same results. To avoid these traps, smart organizations tap their collective and historical experience. Instead of just relying on institutional memory, they have formalized a process for capturing best (and worst) practices. Win or lose, there is always a valuable lesson, and failures can be even more important to remember than successes. Before developing a plan, ensure your team members review lessons learned from previous initiatives and plans. This is the purposeful step of looking at previous debriefs from missions similar to the one we are planning.

Organizations like NASA have entire databases loaded with lessons learned and materials related to such categories as air traffic management, lifting devices, mishap reporting, and personal protective equipment. For example, when you're handling hazardous substances in freezing temperatures, you don't want to relearn a lesson about the decreasing effectiveness of a protective fabric in cold weather. Use lessons someone else has already learned. Good organizational knowledge management can save lives and costs.

Develop a Course of Action

The central element of any plan is the course of action, the actual tasks that must be completed to achieve the goal. It's the principle product that emerges from a team planning session and incorporates the information gathered in the previous steps. Now, do you wait to design the course of action until you have all the information, until you have perfect knowledge? No. One marine colonel observed, "Everyone is always looking for the perfect truth; you never have it. Even if you did have it, the other guy is up to something, so by the time you execute it, your truth isn't perfect anymore."[1] Get as much information as you can, make the best plan possible, and go before you lose the advantage to a competitor. I always prefer an 80 percent plan developed rapidly to a 100 percent plan that takes too long. Having a good process will ensure that you can adjust along the way and bridge that remaining 20 percent.

Key elements of course of action development include:

- **Brainstorming in separate planning teams**. Most people don't contribute their maximum when they're in a large group; there's simply not enough time for everyone to contribute and explain their ideas—especially in squadrons with 14 Type-A personalities competing for air time.

    When you have a large group of participants, break into teams to ensure all your talent has time to shine. Teams may attack the same problem or you may have them each attack different aspects of the plan. I always found it useful to have one team approach a problem while disregarding threats and resource constraints. Sometimes, great ideas would surface in that no-holds-barred planning exercise. When planning in separate groups, I'd

---

[1] David H. Freedman. "Corps Values," *Inc.*, April 4, 1998. www.inc.com/magazine/19980401/906.html.

also impose a 20-minute time limit. The pressure helps groups to work efficiently.

- **Integrating the plans**. When the planning groups come back together, discuss the ideas and suggested tasks developed by each and identify the best ideas to incorporate into the final course of action.

- **Creating the course of action**. A course of action is specific. Its tasks should define who does what, when, what is the desired end result, and how will it be measured. Every action needs a corresponding name, date, and expected outcome. This is a clear, actionable plan.

Before finalizing the course of action, bring in a red team. One reason many corporate planning processes fail to produce desired results is that organizations often lack a culture of red-teaming. During military operations, red teams play the role of adversary; they're the bad guys. But in truth, everyone is on the same team with a shared goal of improving overall performance.

Red teams don't just exist in war games or field exercises. They are a vital component of the military planning process. When one group develops an initial plan, it invites a group of outsiders to review it. The outsiders, the red team, identify potential risks, holes, or contingencies that the original group may have overlooked. It's not an adversarial process, but rather one of professional detachment, all done in the spirit of developing the best possible plans given the organization's goals.

The army believes so strongly in the value of red-teaming that in 2006, they launched the University of Foreign Military and Cultural Studies (UFMCS) at Fort Leavenworth, Kansas. The army began developing the UFMCS concept when studies indicated a growing need to incorporate independent perspectives in its planning process. All levels of the military chain of command needed to ensure plans incorporate modern realities. Planners needed to respond to the new contingencies that emerged on the rapidly-changing, complex global battlespace. Beyond that, how would foreign governments or forces respond to the planned actions? Where were the plan's potential knowledge and execution gaps? The army needed to know.

The new university adds process and structure to the once informal red-teaming process. That's even more important since studies have shown units that employ red teams almost always outperform teams that do not. Red teams trained at the UFMCS will work within army units to challenge assumptions and figures, identify weaknesses, and analyze tactical and strategic options. School graduates will also be knowledgeable about the tactics and capabilities of potential adversaries, so they can add additional value and perspective to the planning process. Red teams give planners the best possible chance for success.

Planning for Operation Iraqi Freedom began in the United States 14 months before H-hour. Since America goes to war as a united front, military strategists representing all services came together to establish a common HDD of what success would look like, then began identifying the effects they hoped to drive. Eventually, their level of planning moved from strategic to tactical, from identifying broad effects to selecting specific targets. They developed multiple courses of action.

Their goal was to neutralize the Iraqi defense system with minimal collateral damage so they explored heavy bombing of airfields, missile sites, and command and control facilities. They discussed knocking out the power grid, as the United States did in the first Gulf War. Or could they think of ways simply to stop pilots and soldiers from getting to work?

Planners developed multiple courses of action then invited uninvolved, unbiased teams to review each one in a red-teaming process called war-gaming. Planners also fed targets, resources, capabilities, and approaches into a computer model that identified risks and generated probabilities for success.

During red-teaming, some argued for attacking military targets first; others pressed to target infrastructure. Some advocated a continuous barrage of bombs and cruise missiles; others argued for a short demonstration followed by a pause during which Iraqi forces could surrender. Eventually, the planners decided upon the best options and developed the final strategies for the invasion of Iraq. Based on command's high level directives, leaders in lower echelons created action plans for individual teams that would ultimately execute the missions that would lead to success or failure. After 14 months of developing, red-teaming, and honing plans, the U.S.-led coalition began the invasion of Iraq on March 20, 2003. Eighteen days after the invasion began, Baghdad fell. The conflict may have dragged on, but the initial battle plan achieved its initial objective of toppling the regime with minimal loss of life.

Servicemen and women understand the high stakes of combat. They share a common mission to serve America and come together to find the best plan. At our firm Afterburner, we believe business is also combat, but few organizations have an environment that can support red-teaming. Smart companies are now educating their people on the process; employees understand how it strengthens the company and eliminates bias. They understand red-teaming isn't personal; it benefits everyone when it's incorporated into an organization's plan. It takes you one step closer to achieving your HDD.

Plan for Contingencies

As the old adage goes, "No plan survives the first contact with the enemy." That's okay because our teams are trained to expect surprises and plan for unexpected situations. Many high-performing military teams use contingency matrices, which spell out triggering events and list the planned response. If trouble comes, they've prepared to the extent possible.

They're ready for the likely or possible threats, know what conditions should trigger a response, and know how to respond. Simple aviation and business examples might be the following:

Contingency	Trigger	Action
Bad weather	Visibility < 1.5 nautical miles; clouds < 500 feet	Use GPS guidance; trail wingman at 2.5 miles
Search engine optimization competition	Top three keywords increase pay-per-click > $5	Use FB and Twitter to communicate prewritten keyword-rich white paper and related concepts/blurbs

Fifteen minutes after they lifted off from Jalalabad Airfield in eastern Afghanistan, two Black Hawk helicopters from the Night Stalkers special operations aviation unit crossed into Pakistan. The flight carried 23 special operators from DEVGRU, the Naval Special Warfare Development Group. Forty-five minutes later, as the Black Hawks were still 45 minutes away from their target, four Chinook helicopters took off from Jalalabad, carrying deadly miniguns and 25 additional DEVGRU SEALs; the two-rotor Chinooks and the SEALs they carried would serve as a backup force should anything go wrong.

Something went wrong as soon as the first helicopter settled toward the night's target, a walled compound in Abbottabad. The practice mock-up in North Carolina had a chain-link fence surrounding it. The actual target in Abbottabad was surrounded by a solid wall which pinned the helicopter's rotor wash inside the compound, causing the aircraft to lose lift. The pilot couldn't recover and crashed the Black Hawk into the compound at an angle that fortunately kept it upright. The SEALs sent a distress call to the Chinooks on standby. One of the Black Hawks was down; the contingency plan automatically went into action. The reserve Chinooks began flying toward Abbottabad.

When they saw the first helicopter crash, the pilots of the second Black Hawk thought that hostile ground fire might have disabled the other aircraft. That triggered another contingency plan. The pilots would not fast-rope their cargo of SEALs into the compound. They automatically vectored to a small adjacent field, just as they'd trained and briefed. From there, the SEALs exited the helicopter and infiltrated the compound. They made their way to the top floor of the central house where their target was most likely hiding.

Shortly after breaching the top floor, the American team encountered the target: a tall man with a long gray beard. Shots were fired. The operators sent a message back to base: "Geronimo, Geronimo, Geronimo. Geronimo E-KIA." They'd achieved their primary objective: Osama bin Laden was no longer a threat.

The team collected intelligence then a portion boarded the remaining Black Hawk. Another group boarded one of the Chinooks that had arrived and another scuttled the downed helicopter. The demolition team placed charges on the helicopter as if it was simply a planned part of the mission. That's because it was; it was a known contingency. Once the charges were set, the last SEALs boarded the Chinook, and the Americans lifted off and returned to base. Every man came home safely because the team had practiced and anticipated contingencies. They knew the raid would not go perfectly and they had identified circumstances that would trigger preplanned actions: sending backup helicopters, landing in an alternate location, or destroying the crippled Black Hawk. It was all part of their planning process.

Few recent military events have been as closely followed as the Abottabad raid, but planning for lower-profile missions or for business is no less important. So let's look at the overall value of smart planning in a business context.

A division of Procter & Gamble (P&G) had spent years developing a new manufacturing process for a special type of paper product. They finally devised the process and commissioned a complex machine that contained a nine-stage oven. A chemical compound was poured into a conveyor belt that carried the compound through the oven. At the end, the hardened material was stamped into the final product. The machine could produce $70,000 of retail value in 24 hours, but the plant managers had trouble developing an oven-cleaning process that would maximize efficiency and reduce cleaning time from 24 hours to 18; long service downtimes were reducing profits.

Working alongside a retired air force general, the factory began to employ a military approach to planning. The manufacturing team had a defined and measurable objective and understood how their production process aligned with P&G's overarching goals, but they'd done a poor job of identifying internal threats. Among the biggest threats was not having the right cleaning equipment staged and ready. One point in the process required forklifts, but the team had not preplanned to ensure the right number of lifts were available. As a result, employees spent precious time finding and acquiring forklifts. The cleaning team also had poor protocols for tracking who was inside the oven itself. Since the oven couldn't be restarted until all cleaning crew members were accounted for, more minutes were lost as people tried to locate missing employees who weren't following protocol. Not addressing these and other threats cost P&G real dollars.

With the exception of missile engineers, military personnel will tell you that our tactics aren't rocket science. Planning to have required resources available or accounting for personnel aren't revolutionary concepts. Sadly for many businesses, however, implementing even obvious solutions can be problematic. That's why employing a carefully developed and deliberate process is vital to success. Planning to mitigate obvious threats is simple, but when companies overlook or fail to execute simple elements of a plan, real losses can occur. Conversely, adopting those simple tactics can lead to great bottom-line improvement.

After revamping their cleaning procedure by preplanning for all needed resources and implementing a better system to track cleaning personnel, the team at P&G sliced the time needed for cleaning in half. Servicing the oven once took 24 hours; it now takes 12, returning $35,000 in value during each cleaning cycle. Since P&G cleans the oven six times each month, they're generating significant new value.

Careful planning and threat management yields results in any sector. And developing an effective process for planning can improve any organization, whether you're focused on consumer products or national defense. Effective planning will align you with your HDD and help you start getting there.

After the planning process ended for my fighter wing or squadron, my team of fighter pilots was squarely aligned behind the HDD set by the air force and the air wing. Our squadron had planned the mission, identified the threats, and selected the targets. Each target had a name by it—each one of us was accountable. It was time to put on our flight suits.

DEVELOPING LEADERS

The military can bring together its greatest minds and develop a strategically sound plan, but success ultimately depends on a group of soldiers taking the right action. In many units, those frontline personnel are under the age of 30, and many are younger than 20. If plans aren't realistically executable by each man and woman in the battlefront unit, you won't achieve your objective. When it comes down to it, ground-level execution is up to the unit leader.

By now, this leader has been indoctrinated and trained. He or she has been oriented to the larger team and focused on group success. Lone wolves or mavericks have become team captains—or washed out. With every step of the personal development process, the military has intentionally developed its people into better leaders by putting them through its regimented and proven processes. During mission planning, this leader advances to the next phase of personal development. He or she plans for combat.

The recent campaigns in Afghanistan aligned with the high-definition destination set by the U.S. government and U.S. Central Command. But within each campaign were countless tactical-level actions and objectives that boiled down to small units executing specific missions to achieve targeted outcomes. National or regional leadership may have developed the larger plans and prepared its units to execute, but every individual mission requires another iteration of the planning process. That unit-level planning process is part of execution, and the military's emerging tactical leaders do their best to eliminate potential execution gaps from the outset.

In the special operations community, officers ranging from 0–3 to 0–5 (lieutenants/captains to commanders/lieutenant colonels) are charged with developing a commander's estimate for each mission. It's their way of confirming they understood an order given to their unit. The commander restates or reviews six things: the situation, the mission, the action on the objective, the execution checklist, communications, and logistics. If the higher-ups approve the commander's estimate, the commander begins planning a course of action brief. His team will study their mission and identify three options—three ways they can achieve the objective. Then they'll use matrices that depict the pros and cons of each option and analyze them all to determine the best route. The commander presents the findings to his superiors and recommends a specific course of action.

If the recommended course of action is approved, the commander and his unit begin developing the mission concept, which spells out the next level of tactical detail. The plan goes through another approval cycle and the unit then designs the patrol leader's orders, the last level of mission detail. Based on the patrol leader's orders, the team rehearses the mission and waits for the order to go. Interestingly, because of the deep trust that develops between all members of a special operations unit, officers will often have enlisted men write the commander's estimate or other sections of a plan or set of patrol leader's orders. If a petty officer or sergeant is the expert sniper, he'll often receive responsibility for planning a surgical shooting mission. The military is constantly developing leaders at all levels and ranks.

Not all missions have the luxury of long planning cycles. If a Taliban rocket-propelled grenade disables a U.S. helicopter, a team of Green Berets or Rangers might have only 15 minutes to develop a plan before they're inbound to the crash site. In those instances, trust among team members becomes paramount. The commander will disperse responsibility into planning cells. Certain members plan the insertion and extraction, identifying the vehicles or aircraft needed to get the team to and from the crash site. Others identify the weapons and equipment needed on the ground, while yet another group will identify which personnel with which skillsets need to accompany the team on the mission.

Young leaders on elite teams develop experience by planning. They earn responsibility for parts of a mission, with those parts growing more significant over time as they prove their abilities and earn the confidence of team members. The nuts-and-bolts of planning truly teach leadership. Officers are designing actions that may get some of their men killed; exercising that responsibility forges judgment and respect rapidly.

Sometimes people think of leadership as rallying troops on a battlefield or energizing employees at an annual meeting. Certainly, those can be great venues to join people to your cause, but often leadership involves doing the unglamorous work that makes a team successful. Here's the great thing though. When that tough, unseen work earns widespread trust and leads to success, both the leader and the led have more confidence, more *courage to execute.*

MISSION CHECKLIST

Plan Your Mission

1. Determine the mission objective.
   a. Is it clear?
   b. Is it measurable?
   c. Is it achievable?
   d. Does it align with your HDD?
2. Identify the threats.
   a. Identify external threats and whether they are controllable or uncontrollable.
   b. Identify internal threats and whether they are controllable or uncontrollable.
3. Identify your available resources.
4. Evaluate lessons learned.
5. Develop a course of action.
   a. Work in teams to brainstorm to create action steps.
   b. Red-team.
   c. Develop a final plan with who, what, and when.
6. Plan for contingencies.
   a. Determine potential contingency triggers.
   b. Clearly plan a response action for each trigger.

CHAPTER 5

BATTLE RHYTHM: ON TRACK, ON TARGET, AND ON TIME

During Vietnam, the ratio of U.S.-to-enemy aircraft downed fell precipitously and the military recognized an execution gap. They hypothesized that their pilots needed better instruction in aerial combat. The navy developed its TOPGUN aviation training program at Naval Air Station (NAS) Miramar (now Marine Corps Air Station Miramar) outside San Diego and the air force enhanced its Fighter Weapons School at Nellis Air Force Base in Nevada. The school at Nellis became known as the Fighter Weapons Instructor Course, as the air force aimed to train pilots who could in turn train others. Now simply called the Weapons Instructor Course, the program has taught air force pilots air-to-air and air-to-ground tactics—and equipped its graduates to bring the lessons home to their squadrons. Graduates are called instructors or patch-wearers, and are highly-regarded. Jim Demarest finished the four-month-long program first in his class.

"We'd have 30 or 32 rides during the course," Demarest explained, "and each one lasted about an hour. But the preparation and briefing beforehand could take up to four hours, and the debrief after could go even longer, so you were looking at some long days. When you only have an hour aloft in the aircraft, the briefing is one of the most critical parts of the mission."[1]

Before each hop, an instructor plans the entire flight profile. He or she plans the taxi and takeoff, including which runway they will use and whether they will take off together in formation or individually. The instructor plots the ingress route to the airspace, the specific maneuvers each flight will perform, and the route they'll take home. That includes speeds, altitudes, and formations. For air-to-air maneuvers, the instructor might design a scenario where the student is 9,000 feet behind the lead, flying at 450 knots at an altitude of 15,000 feet, heading due north. When the lead calls "Fight's on," the student's task is to close on the instructor and take a simulated missile shot. Instructors come up with similar detail for each of the maneuvers they have planned. They routinely spend 25 percent of their briefing time before the flight discussing contingency scenarios. Since nothing ever goes

---

[1]James Demarest. Interview with the author, August 18, 2013.

according to plan, detailed planning for contingencies prepares a pilot to react quickly and safely if certain situations emerge.

Instructors take all relevant information about the flight and brief the student. That starts with prepping the briefing room. To prepare a briefing room, they lay out maps, checklists, and diagrams to discuss with the student. On whiteboards, they'll list out maneuvers and weapons. They use the same room for almost every flight, ensuring students get serious every time they walk into that room; it sets the tone for a successful brief. Students know each preflight brief begins exactly two hours before their scheduled flight and lasts for 70 minutes. Then it's step to the jets. The format and timing of each briefing never changes. That consistency makes for powerfully focused and highly effective communication tool.

"It's very important to get every possible ounce of value out of a flight," Demarest explains. "Experience shows that a good preparation and a good briefing yield success during execution in a big way. Poor prep and a poor briefing will waste training time in the air and lower your overall situational awareness. And you'll most likely end up on the receiving end of a beating."

BRIEFING

Just as the military turns 18-year-old recruits into contributing members of high performance teams, it turns 22-year-old college graduates into the world's finest pilots, although it'll take years before they're ready for Weapons Instructor School and can become instructors like Jim Demarest. Remember, the military combats complexity with simplicity, and every branch of service has developed a simple process that eases a new officer from a classroom into an aircraft cockpit, the first step toward becoming an elite pilot.

Before flying the first training mission, a new pilot always briefs with an instructor. For their entire careers, pilots will brief before every flight they ever take, no matter how many missions they have under their belts. And it doesn't matter whether the mission is for training or for combat. For training briefings, new pilots and their instructors will sit together in a quiet room with no distractions, where they can focus without interruption; these briefs run longer than typical briefs in active squadrons. A detailed map usually occupies the room's table or desk, and instructor and student walk through the flight, identifying landmarks and threats. They plan their turns and their altitude changes. They plan for emergencies. They plan for mistakes.

From experience, I can tell you that later in your flying career, when you're flying at 500 knots, you don't have time to think about your response to a threat; you have to respond instantly. A good brief for a seasoned pilot usually includes an example of a real mishap to remind us that flying is dangerous business. We can get overconfident and forget that many of our regulations are written in blood; we have them because someone died. We can't afford to forget that at any stage of our career.

As a lieutenant, I was flying my F-15 in an adversary role, playing the role of a MiG-29. I was the "bandit," flying solo and battling a flight of two other F-15s in simulated air-to-air combat. It was a good day and I downed both F-15s in the first of our three engagements using simulated air-to-air weapons. In the second engagement, I "killed" one with a mock missile shot and outmaneuvered the other. For measurement reasons, one of the F-15s needed to "kill" me in the last engagement and with fuel running low and egos running on octane, the pressure was on. We were in a mature engagement—we'd gone through a number of high-G turns—and I was in a defensive position, trying to shake the F-15 on my tail. He could never get a clear shot, so the second F-15 re-entered the fight and broke a major rule of engagement: An engaged fighter owns the area behind a bandit. The second F-15 flew into the cone behind me and collided with the jet on my six, my tail. One pilot ejected and I escorted the other F-15 to a nearby airport. Neither that damaged F-15 nor its at fault pilot ever flew again. I learned as a young lieutenant that procedures, policies, and checklists exist for a reason. Always follow them.

Corporate business doesn't always need to move at Mach 1 for briefing to be important. Imagine going into a major client meeting without a script or a plan. Forward-thinking companies will stage briefings at the beginning of a new project, or perhaps on a quarterly basis. Sometimes, team members will brief before a particular meeting. After a briefing, your production workers, your salespeople, and your managers should be ready to execute the task at hand and be able to respond rapidly and correctly to changing conditions. You're aligned. Now you're ready to prepare for the execution phase.

Briefing is the second step in the Flawless Execution engine: *Plan, brief, execute, debrief.* It's absolutely vital in communicating your plan to the team members who you'll hold accountable for implementing that plan. They need to understand who does what, when, and what you expect as the outcome. To ensure alignment around the overall plan, it's critical that we plan using the six-step process discussed earlier, then brief the plan before we execute it.

Briefing establishes and demonstrates leadership while also developing leaders. Standing before your seated squadron mates and leading a briefing gets you used to command and lets others see you as a leader.

A good briefing establishes organization and discipline, and it sets a tone of seriousness; the time for jokes is over. It empowers the audience to become part of the team and mission. A sloppy brief guarantees sloppy execution, which almost always ensures you'll fail to achieve your mission objectives.

From a communication perspective, briefing ensures that the individuals who will execute the plan understand their responsibilities. One last time, they take note of how other people will depend on their actions. They review their expected actions and goals. They make sure they have all the knowledge they need.

Finally, we brief to transition from planning to execution. Collaborative planning has generated the best possible course of action; many viewpoints and ideas have been openly considered. Now, however, time for discussion and respectful argument has passed. The team has decided on its course of action and debate is over. The leader's brief ensures everyone now accepts his or her authority and understands the expectations they must meet in order for the mission to succeed. The brief unifies and aligns the team around the plan. Everyone should now be on board.

A successful brief needs the right environment; we call it a micro-climate for success. It includes setting, preparation, and organization. Before every mission, my squadron met in our briefing room (our navy counterparts call them *ready rooms*) and sat through a briefing that explained who, what, and when, as well as the intended outcomes and metrics. In the squadron hangar, we'd been talking and joking, but when we stepped into the briefing room, all that changed. We were in an environment that called for seriousness.

The room would be clean and neat, maps would be laid out, as would visual references. That told us the flight leader had prepared well in advance and that built confidence in the brief. Nothing empowers a team more than seeing a well-prepared, well-thought out brief. We believed our leader was in charge and understood the mission. All that started with good preparation on the part of the briefer. The simple things—ensuring tables and chairs are set up, having hand-outs ready, prepping whiteboards—go a long way in instilling confidence in a team. Rooms should be prepped and ready, just like the leader.

When I led a brief, I made sure to outline the content of my brief and was prepared to field questions at the end. Usually, I'd pass out a written outline as a final aide to the team. After the planning process, everyone should understand the plan, but this was my last opportunity to make sure. Since I wanted their attention and respect, I made it a point to arrive on time and have the room set up properly. Again, in the military, we believe in the basics. We also made sure every brief followed a standard routine, which helps the briefer and the team; everyone knows what to expect.

The same process that worked in the air force has worked in business as well. Briefs may be about complex battle plans or simple daily plans. Many businesses have adopted daily briefings where they'll recap daily, weekly, monthly, or annual goals and metrics. Good leaders always communicate information central to success of the organization. People at all levels want to know how they fit into the big picture; they want to be part of the overall team's success. Use the briefing to remind them of their role and contribution.

Your brief may be short or long, but it should follow a standard format. In our squadrons, we followed a format with five components. I call it briefing to win, and like anyone steeped in military culture, I use an acronym: BRIEF.

1. **Brief the scenario**. Create situational awareness by placing the mission in context of the organization's larger goals. A good brief will reinforce team alignment and remind everyone of their role's importance.

2. **Review the mission objectives**. Focus the team on the objective and the intended effect of the mission. Remember that objectives should be clear, measurable, achievable, and aligned with the organization's high-definition destination (HDD).

3. **Identify the threats and resources**. Every operation has countless threats, but reiterate the primary threats to mission success and the resources available to counter them.

4. **Execution (courses of action)**. Review *who* does *what, when*. No need to be complicated; state the facts and reiterate the responsibilities.

5. **Flexibility (contingencies)**. Identify the triggers that will alert us that a contingency or uncontrollable threat is occurring, and review the steps the team has agreed it will take to manage it. If X happens, I do Y and you do Z; there's no time to ask questions in the heat of battle. Clear triggers will prevent inaction and make sure the team or the responsible parties address contingencies immediately to keep the mission on course.

Success often stems from attention to details, and briefers should remember three key points. First, briefings are *not* meetings. Discussions should have already occurred; this is a one-way conversation. Second, don't field any questions until the brief ends, and third, use visual aids whenever possible.

I've seen companies and military units go straight from planning to executing. I can tell you that briefing is absolutely vital to Flawless Execution. *Do not undervalue this step*. It's part of the preparation that gives military teams the confidence and courage to execute. If you brief the plan effectively, and on a regular and consistent basis, your team's level of execution will increase considerably.

When the briefing ended, it was go-time. We each grabbed our helmet, strapped on our parachute harness, and stepped to the jets. Several minutes later our engines were cranking. Then we had to execute.

EXECUTION RHYTHM

Execute is the third phase of the Flawless Execution engine: *Plan, brief, execute, debrief.* If you're a SEAL, this is where you put on your tank and fins and leave the submarine for the shore. If you're a Thunderbird pilot, this is when you man your jet. If you're a Ranger, this is when you parachute behind enemy lines. Execution is combat.

Missions, like businesses, have a cyclical nature to them, a natural rhythm. It takes time to plan a mission, brief the participants, conduct the mission, and then debrief it so the lessons learned are passed along to others before the cycle repeats. During World War II that cycle occurred over perhaps five days. A commander would order an air strike then squadrons would prepare propeller-driven heavy bombers for long missions. After the bombing mission, reconnaissance planes would assess the damage. Only then would planners work on the next mission. A week's time might have passed from planning to final assessment.

By Operation Desert Storm in 1991, the cycle was down to a mere 12 hours if not less, with half of those missions being flown at night. Night-vision goggles and advanced technology let operations run as well at night as they did during the day. Today, battle rhythm is ever faster. It's so time-compressed that a mission might be measured in minutes. An aircraft carrier can launch F/A-18 pilots who can react instantly to a data link from a Predator drone piloted from Nevada, strike a target in Afghanistan, assess battle damage, and reset themselves in the air. And all the moving parts can keep up. The ground crews have the aircraft ready to launch, controllers are managing the air space, and the carrier or base is ready for the jets to return. When the team has rhythm, all of the components of a mission come together and lead to successful execution.

During the Cuban Missile Crisis in 1962, our nation's war readiness posture was elevated to DEFCON 2, the highest state of military readiness short of actual war. Nearly every bomber and fighter in the United States Air Force was fueled, armed, and moved to an alert pad or to their designated dispersal base in the United States or overseas. Strategic Air Command bases were packed with pilots, copilots, bombers, navigators, and all of the crew members and maintainers. Air force fighter and bomber wings were moved around the United States like chess pieces, the fighters to the south, the bombers to the north. Strategic Air Command alone put in 109,000 hours of flight time including 4,076 aerial refuelings. They kept 75 heavy bombers flying counter-clockwise patterns around the North Pole, continuously, 24 hours a day. They had a total of 2,952 nuclear weapons loaded and 1,436 bombers on hair-trigger, 15-minute ground alert. Dozens of civilian airports received B-47s and hundreds more were flown to overseas bases. Twenty million miles were flown by the bombers alone; hundreds of fighter pilots sat on alert with hundreds more on combat air patrols. Despite the staggering level of activity, only five accidents occurred.[2]

Everyone had been trained to do their specific job, and despite the enormous difference in backgrounds, they could execute as part of a multifaceted complex organization in a complex, tense environment. Across the breadth of the entire air force, hundreds of thousands of people were moving in harmony to achieve the desired intended effect with scarcely a misstep. That's excellence at the highest level. That's training. That's battle rhythm.

Execution rhythm is more than battle rhythm. It coordinates the pace of activity using an additional component: process. Execution rhythm is the pace set by the *plan-brief-execute-debrief* cycle of the Flawless Execution engine. It's the metabolism of a healthy organization.

---

[2]Douglas Keeney. *15 Minutes: General Curtis LeMay and the Countdown to Nuclear Annihilation*. New York: Macmillan, 2012.

Note that it's not the metabolism of a healthy unit or department. To have execution rhythm, you need to view the organization holistically. It's a system greater than the sum of its parts. That's why you should be careful when using different management techniques; too often, methods don't focus on the entire picture and will generate subpar results. It's like a coach or coxswain focusing on a single rower in an eight-person crew. Only when each crewmember is properly trained, coached, and directed will the scull move through the water straight and smooth. Each rower pulls and feathers in unison, exerting just the right amount of power to balance the pulls on the opposite side. As a pilot, I see execution rhythm in a well-run integrated combat turn (ICT) at my fighter wing. ICTs test our wing's battle readiness by seeing how many sorties we can launch in a finite amount of time. It tests how efficiently our entire wing can plan, brief, execute, and debrief. A good rating depends on developing a plan and launching aircraft—then the real challenge starts. Returning fighters radio ahead with fuel, repair, and armament needs. Maintainers must have the right weapons, right amount of fuel, and right parts and repair tools on the ramp when the plane returns. I'd stay in the cockpit as they readied my F-15 for another hop; an intelligence officer would debrief me at the jet. It was like being in a NASCAR pit. As soon as every team had finished its job, I'd takeoff on the next mission of the ICT cycle. When we did it well, it was a beautiful rhythm, because it was not just my F-15 and me being "turned"; it was the entire fighter wing with all of our jets, departments, and personnel moving in a 24/7 typed cadence to test our combat readiness. Throw in simulated chemical attacks where we all must don our protective "chem gear" and the level of difficulty jumps tenfold.

From experience, we've identified five aspects of execution rhythm:

1. Leadership
2. Simplicity
3. Cyclical process
4. Discipline
5. Learning through experience

Leadership is the coxswain in the eight-man rowing scull; it's the Ranger squad leader; it's the air wing commander. Without leadership, alignment won't happen or only takes place haphazardly. Ideally, rhythm cascades from headquarters down to field commanders, who synch their operations with their commanders and peers. Rhythm may change with battlefield conditions, but regardless, it provides the chain of command with a foundation, the basis for coordinating and synchronizing operations. It determines how quickly the *plan-brief-execute-debrief* cycle occurs. When the pace of battle increases—or when a competitor brings new pressure to bear—the rhythm speeds up. Adaptable teams will begin planning and executing in a more rapid cycle, and that cyclical nature is the second component of execution rhythm. Remember when, in Chapter 4, we discussed how Colonel Boyd developed the OODA loop and aimed to get inside the observe-orient-decide-act loop of his adversary? This is the same principle. The unit with the shortest and most effective execution rhythm wins.

In a modern battle operation, complexity will kill you. Perhaps literally. Execution rhythm is simplicity. There may be countless moving parts, numerous contingencies, infinite decision points, but effective organizations streamline everything so their people can execute. Every participant focuses on the duties most important to them and their actions. Execution rhythm is that simple baseline that keeps an organization moving toward its HDD.

Just like music rhythm has repetition, so does execution rhythm. Good rhythm simplifies complex processes into repeatable tasks, which lend themselves to mastery. Repetition empowers a team to hone its process to near-perfection, as it allows members to make slight adjustments each cycle. Thus the organization creeps closer to its HDD with each repetition of the execution cycle.

To have execution rhythm, an organization needs discipline. Not only do people need to understand their specific and simplified roles, they need to focus on them. They can't allow distractions or their own predilections to take them off task. An effectively executing organization works in concert.

Good rhythm learns as it goes. Organizations that execute rhythmically incorporate lessons across iterative execution cycles, improving themselves in a seamless way as they continue executing and performing at high levels. They have feedback mechanisms that let them evaluate their progress and performance, and they are diligent about adjusting themselves to be more effective.

CHECKPOINTS

When future Admiral Jack Towers took off from Rockaway Beach, New York, in 1919, he aimed to complete the first transatlantic flight. His HDD was landing safely in Europe, on time and on target, with his flight of three Navy Curtiss flying boats. Nobody had ever flown across the Atlantic. This pioneering aviator planned to fly from New York to Newfoundland then to the Azores before finally landing in Plymouth, England.

Navigation tools did not exist for such a long flight over the Atlantic, so the navy deployed a long line of destroyers along the course, each with a signal beacon. The three flying boats followed the destroyers, clicking off checkpoint after checkpoint, ensuring they remained on course over the vast ocean. Importantly, the navy had spaced the ships at relatively close distances to ensure the planes did not drift off course early in the mission. Small discrepancies near New York would become magnified as the planes continued east; being one-half mile off over the North American coastline could, if uncorrected, push the planes hundreds of miles off course over the mission's duration. As it turned out, the destroyers did their job—until the weather intervened.

During the long Newfoundland-to-Azores leg, the conditions deteriorated and the flight became separated as it flew through a storm system. Two planes ditched. Waves swamped one and the crew was quickly rescued. The second plane, ditched by Towers himself, was subsequently crippled by the rough seas. Its radio also malfunctioned. The storm had blown them off course and nobody knew where to look. Jack Towers began sailing his stricken plane through the waves toward the Azores, with the storm battering the now-flightless craft more with every passing hour. In an impressive display of seamanship, survival, and celestial navigation, Towers literally sailed his plane across 200 miles of ocean and into the harbor at San Miguel in the Azores. The trip took 53 hours. The following week, the original trio's last serviceable flying boat completed the mission.

The end state did not look how Towers had originally envisioned. He'd started out following his checkpoints, monitoring his progress, but when conditions suddenly changed, he was blown off-course. He had to improvise and adapt. But he was prepared. He had the necessary skills and mettle, and by having three aircraft in his flight, he improved his odds that at least one would accomplish the mission objective: to make an American serviceman the first person to cross the Atlantic by air.

You can say that Towers completed his mission objective more so than reaching a larger HDD; for instance, the HDD, in this case, could be a higher vision set by the navy for its aviation program. Either way, he experienced unexpected changes, just like every business experiences. The key for aviators and businesses alike is being prepared and able to adapt. Towers worked his way back toward those guiding checkpoints that he knew would lead him to his destination. In that same way, checkpoints will keep you on course, or get you back on course, and help to track toward your original plan. Thus, it's important to incorporate checkpoints as you plan, so set incremental goals by which you can judge your progress. Including these in your plans ensures you'll advance toward your ultimate vision.

TASK SATURATION

Execution rhythm has an enemy. Great teams aspire to perform at high levels and dedicate themselves to doing everything correctly. But sometimes, these high performers get overwhelmed; they're tracking too many variables or managing too many actions. Teams or individuals can become so inundated with tasks or information, or become so channelized on one thing, that they lose their ability to execute. In aviation, we call this task saturation and it can be deadly.

On December 29, 1972, Eastern Airlines Flight 401 out of New York began its approach to Miami International Airport and the pilots lowered the landing gear. Only two of the three positive indicator lights illuminated, telling them one of the gears, the nose gear, had not deployed, or that the warning system had malfunctioned. The crew put the plane on autopilot at a constant altitude while they tried to solve the problem. Inadvertently, one of the men nudged the control yoke enough to disengage the autopilot. The plane began a slow descent at a barely-noticeable rate of 200 feet per minute. The pilots became so focused on the landing gear indicator light that they failed to check their attitude indicator or altitude indicator, either of which would have immediately warned them of the plane's dilemma. When they finally noticed the altitude, they were less than 100 feet above the Florida Everglades. Twelve seconds later, 99 people died because both pilots were distracted by what turned out to be a burned-out lightbulb. Never let yourself or your team lose sight of where you are relative to your objective and your threats.

I've told that story for years because it's such a sobering and powerful reminder of how even great pilots, or great businesspeople, can become disoriented. The Eastern Airlines pilots lost track of their altitude because they became task saturated. We call that the silent killer to good execution. It's the moment you have too much to do and not enough time or resources to do it, and you lose focus on the most important thing. When you become task saturated, errors increase and performance decreases. The U.S. airline industry hasn't had a major disaster like Flight 401 in more than 30 years, in part because of the safeguards and new procedures implemented after the accident investigation. But it doesn't mean task saturation is gone.

Two of my air force friends flew perfectly good aircraft into the ground not too long ago because they got so focused on the wrong thing that they lost all situational awareness. If I had asked them how they were doing 10 seconds before impact, they would have said, "A-OK." It's called dying relaxed. Were my friends good pilots? They were *great* pilots, but they got so busy tracking bogeys, maneuvering, and watching their systems that they lost track of their positions.

You can become so task saturated that you channel all your attention onto one thing, and you have no idea you're about to crash your aircraft. Even the best-trained pilots in the world can lose track of the ground.

What's the ground in your business? If you're an entrepreneur, you might become so focused on winning a key contract that you neglect a problem in your manufacturing process. Since closing deals is usually more exciting than fixing process headaches, it's easy to lose focus on the manufacturing problem. You tell yourself that you'll fix it tomorrow, but the tomorrows come and go. Consequently, when you close that contract, you won't be able to fulfill it. You might as well have flown into the ground. Financial planners risk paying attention to their largest mature client at the expense of rapidly growing young clients. Legal teams can become so fixated on one element of a case that they overlook valuable evidence or other avenues that could lead to resolution. You get the idea.

Unfortunately, runaway complexity and rapid pace have made task saturation the top obstacle to effective execution in corporate America. It's the prime culprit behind America's execution problem. Some hard-charging workers wear it like a badge of honor—when they say they're busy, they feel important—but it can ruin a project, a team, or a company. Task saturation leads to errors and low performance. One task-saturated surgeon, one overwhelmed pilot, one overworked engineer can kill an organization's reputation and even cost human lives. When people become task saturated, they either quit, compartmentalize, or channel. In each case, their performance deteriorates rapidly. Quitters stop working or stop being productive. Those who compartmentalize appear busy but focus on tasks that accomplish little. Most of us, however, channel our focus onto one thing and ignore the rest. None of those behaviors leads to a good outcome.

Let's go back to the special operations mission at Paitilla Airport in Panama, where SEAL Team 4 went after Manuel Noriega's private jet. The night's results and the 12 casualties sustained by the assault team highlighted the value of creating a high-definition destination and then letting on-the-ground commanders make tactical decisions. The mission also emphasized the dangers of task saturation.

As the SEALs crossed the open airfield and neared the hangar where Noriega's jet sat, Panamanian Defense Forces ambushed them. The first round of gunfire hit four SEALs. The surviving members then became so channelized on caring for their downed comrades that they forgot the first rule of a firefight: win the firefight first. In rendering aid to their downed buddies, they lost focus on their primary objective (subduing the enemy, completing the mission, and disabling the jet). Eight more SEALs were wounded before the operation ended. The mission parameter of minimal collateral damage went out the window once the bullets started flying. SEALs used every weapon they had. A rocket destroyed the jet and grenades nearly destroyed the hangar.[3]

The tragic mission resulted in heavy debriefing and review by the special operation command. The debriefs and investigation showed that command had become so focused on minimizing collateral damage and civilian casualties that it needlessly placed the SEALs at risk by sending them on such a close-range mission without adequate support or sufficient preemptive attacks to soften up the defenders. On the ground, the SEAL team became so channelized on tending to the first four wounded men that they stopped concentrating on the most important thing—the mission objective. They also lost track of their biggest threat—the Panamanian Defense Force. They lost situational awareness. The team leader could have ended the mission at any time, but the group and leadership had become overly fixated on completing a mission that had already been compromised by, first, a decision from headquarters, and, second, unexpected resistance and casualties. The lessons of the Paitilla mission had a tremendous and lasting impact on the special operations community.

I'll say it again: We live in a complex, fast-moving world, and few things move faster than an F-15. I've been at 10,000 feet, at 600 knots, in bad weather, with more than 100 instruments that I need to scan, radio calls to deal with, mountains below me, a wingman in formation next to me, a target approaching, weapons to launch, and no idea

[3]Melissa Healy, "Tactics Switch May Have Boosted Navy's Invasion Toll," *Los Angeles Times*, January 27, 1990. http://articles.latimes.com/1990-01-27/news/mn-625_1_panama-invasion.

when an adversary aircraft will appear. You bet I'm a candidate for task saturation. But we combat complexity with simplicity and process.

In the air, we have our own processes for avoiding task saturation, namely task shedding, cross-checks, and checklists. First, we'll try to reassign some tasks from the bottom of our priority list, and often a wingman with extra capacity will help. Since we're in alignment with our HDD, we take care not to shed tasks that are critical to our mission. Many military teams plan well in advance to help members task-shed at various points during a mission. A special forces demolition expert may have many roles on a mission, but when the time arrives for him to plant and arm an explosive device, he sheds all other duties. His team members anticipate this transfer of duty and they defend the perimeter, manage communications, and plot their exit so the demolition expert can concentrate fully on the most important task at hand, the one for which he is uniquely trained. Once he sets the charge, he'll resume his other duties. Same thing goes for a flight when one aircraft needs to focus on targeting while the others manage hostile aircraft.

Our second defense against task saturation is our habit of cross-checking. Pilots are trained to monitor our most important instruments, always tracking our position relative to our greatest threat. In a fighter cockpit, the attitude indicator is often the most important instrument and we're always most wary of the ground. That's what can kill us.

As a pilot, I always check the attitude indicator when I'm airborne. That central gauge is my home base. No matter how good or bad the conditions outside the cockpit, I'm always cross-checking my gauges and displays—those key providers of situational awareness. I start with my attitude indicator, which gives my position relative to the earth's horizon: Is the ground getting nearer or farther? Using the hub-and-spoke model we discussed in Chapter 3, I check attitude, then airspeed, then recheck attitude before checking altitude. I stay focused on the most important thing, my position relative to the biggest threat: the ground.

A fighter cockpit has hundreds of instruments and switches to monitor, and when I'm flying through a clear sky at 40,000 feet, I can

monitor most of them over time. Cross-checking really gets important when the weather deteriorates and I'm flying below 2,000 feet or
approaching a target. We call those critical phases of flight. In those
phases, I can only focus on five or six key instruments. I task-shed the
others. I've trained to identify what those key instruments are ahead
of time, before I ever stepped into the aircraft.

Businesses also encounter critical phases of flight. Too often, employees are trying to do everything they normally do when in fact they need
to focus their energy on only one or two critical areas, the things that
are most important to the business's ability to make it through this critical phase. Corporate planners need to identify and communicate the
key metrics for employees to monitor and the key tasks on which they
should focus when those important phases arise. Planning and preparing before you fly into your critical phases of flight is imperative.

No matter how long we've been flying, no matter how big our
egos may be, pilots always carry checklists, our third defense. Checklists are one of the most basic and effective ways to fight task saturation. Simplicity combats complexity, and nothing is more simple
than a checklist—nor is anything more effective. Missing a step in a
landing sequence can be deadly, but crosschecking off each item as
you approach the runway ensures you and your jet are ready to be
gear-down.

But even with checklists, errors still occur. A C-17 Globemaster
III was approaching Bagram Airfield in Afghanistan during 2009, and
the pilots lined the big transport up perfectly with the designated runway. They were busy with landing procedures and, as the plane settled
toward the airstrip, they readied themselves for yet another routine
landing. Instead of settling gently onto its landing gear, however, the
aircraft's belly suddenly began scraping along the runway as smoke and
sparks flew from beneath the fuselage. The pilots had failed to lower
the landing gear.

The investigation cited several causes, including task saturation. The
primary cause, however, was simply the crew's failure to lower the gear
as required by the Before Landing checklist. Checklists prevent mishaps.
Simplicity combats complexity.

In some cases, checklists can salvage a mission otherwise doomed to fail.

In 1970, naval aviator Jim Lovell found himself in command of a nearly-dead spacecraft, 200,000 miles away from Earth. *Apollo 13* had lost fuel, oxygen, and battery power and, quietly, many engineers at NASA thought Lovell and his crew would never return. *Apollo 13* could become NASA's greatest disaster. Flight director Gene Kranz would not give up, and the film *Apollo 13* famously depicts him instructing his teams, "Failure is not an option." Kranz didn't give up, nor did the astronauts trapped in the crippled spacecraft. Jim Lovell, Fred Haise, and Jack Swigert, remained calm. They focused on solving one problem, then another. They realized they would become overwhelmed and hopelessly defeated if they considered every single step and obstacle that stood between them and a safe return; considered all at once, the challenges seemed insurmountable. The astronauts focused on one checklist item after another, thinking about the next item only when it was time. For them as well as for mission control, failure was not an option and the crew enforced strict mental discipline and relied on a familiar process so they could fix their problems one by one and survive.

Adrift in space, the crew had shut down the power in their spacecraft to conserve energy so they might have enough battery power left to safely reenter the Earth's atmosphere. The essentially dead ship's inertia carried it toward the Moon, where the physicists in Mission Control knew gravity would sling the spacecraft around and put it back on a return trajectory. When *Apollo 13* rounded the moon, Lovell executed a short engine burn to adjust their course. They again shut down the spacecraft and began a long and uncertain journey home.

NASA knew that the spacecraft's batteries were almost entirely drained, so they called astronaut Ken Mattingly, who was originally slated to fly the mission, and put him in a simulator. He was charged with figuring out how to bring *Apollo 13* back to life with the limited power available. The incorrect power-up sequence would overload the nearly depleted batteries and doom the astronauts. Mattingly sat in the simulator for hours, trying sequence after sequence, failing again and again.

Fortunately, when time arrived for reentry, Mattingly and NASA had developed a precise checklist for powering up the command module, which would carry the three-person crew back through the atmosphere. If Lovell and his crew executed a procedure out-of-sequence or skipped a step, they wouldn't have enough power to maneuver for reentry. The pilots of *Apollo 13* could easily have become task-saturated or overwhelmed by their situation. In the end, three of America's most accomplished pilots used a simple checklist to bring their spacecraft back to life and line up for reentry. That list saved their lives and brought *Apollo 13* home safely. For them, it was no different than landing a jet on a runway; they had always used checklists because checklists combat task saturation. Checklists make sure you get home. Simplicity combats complexity.

For 25 years, military aviators used several informal checklists, but still relied more on pilot ability and knowledge than on strict procedures. That changed in 1935, with the crash of a prototype Boeing B-17 Flying Fortress, the famous heavy bomber that would darken the skies over Germany during World War II. The B-17 prototype had four engines and was a significantly more complex aircraft than the military had ever seen. Boeing had designed the bomber to meet new army specifications and in tests it performed marvelously. Then as Congress was evaluating the aircraft, the B-17's highly seasoned test pilots made a simple mistake.

On October 30, 1935, the prototype lifted off from Wright Field in Ohio. At 300 feet, the crew knew something was wrong. The nose kept angling up, far steeper than it should have been. The pilots couldn't correct the steepening angle and the plane stalled, it lost all lift. It crashed back to earth. The accident report ruled out all systems failure and instead concluded that the elevator control had been locked. Essentially, pilot error was to blame. How could a team of professional pilots make such a simple mistake like failing to unlock one of the plane's most important control surfaces?

With the growing complexity of aircraft, the military realized even their best men could make mistakes when confronted with the dizzying number of procedures and checks needed before takeoff and landing.

The pilots at Boeing developed a nine-step checklist for the B-17, which the crew used at the next Congressional demonstration. The crew flew the mission as planned and the military approved full production. That successful flight gave the army air force one of its most important tools to affect critical leverage points far behind German lines. The army institutionalized the use of checklists after that 1935 crash, and checklists have remained indispensable components of aviation ever since. They're what gave pilots the courage to fly over oceans during World War II, they're what gave Jim Lovell the confidence to bring *Apollo 13* home, and they're what give modern pilots the confidence to take off in the world's most advanced aircraft.

Industries outside aviation are just now recognizing the beauty and effectiveness of simple checklists like those used by the military. They empower teams and build discipline. They give every team member the authority to prevent errors.

Surgeons in many American hospitals now use similar checklists before they operate on patients. The lead surgeon reads a checklist with the patient's name and details about the procedure. Before the surgeon makes any incisions, the surgical nurse must respond affirmatively to every item on the list. Surgeons are generally as self-confident as pilots, but they too see the value of simple checklists. In surgery, the list empowers the nurse to ensure the safety of the patient. It momentarily equalizes the authority of doctor and nurse to protect the patient's well-being. One international study led by Harvard School of Public Health professor Dr. Atul Gawande and published in the *New England Journal of Medicine* observed that using checklists improved patient survival rates by 47 percent, and reduced the rate of complications by 37 percent.[4]

"We were not anticipating such a dramatic reduction," said Gawande. "We had initially planned the size of the study to pick up a 15 percent reduction in complications." Dr. Gawande also related a story where an anesthesiologist read a presurgery checklist and realized

---

[4]Maia Szalavitz, "Study: A Simple Surgery Checklist Saves Lives," *Time*, January 14, 2009.

extra blood might be needed—but the team did not have an adequate supply in the operating room. Before the procedure began, the team acquired the necessary blood which they did in fact need during surgery. "I'm convinced that the fact that the anesthesiologist caught that was what saved this man's life," Dr. Gawande said. A similar study conducted in Michigan showed checklist use helped reduce infections by 66 percent. That saved lives—along with $175 million.[5]

The study also reported that "to implement the checklist, all test sites had to introduce a formal pause in care during surgery for pre-operative team introductions and briefings and postoperative debrief-ings."[6] Each of those practices has been shown to improve safety and attitudes while reducing rates of death or complication by up to 80 percent!

No matter how proficient or talented the surgical team, checklists can still improve performance. There are also times when pilots get overwhelmed and we need a first officer or navigator to double-check us. If they see we missed a step in a takeoff or landing checklist, they're empowered to point it out. In task-saturated environments, lists save lives and prevent costly mishaps.

"With a checklist, you set the standard without having to say it directly," explains U.S. Marine Corps aviator Andrew Dingee. "The military brings discipline to that standardization. You can say it's invaluable. I can also tell you exactly what lack of discipline or standardization can cause. Try $5 million per mistake, in some cases."

As a Marine Corps Harrier pilot Dingee received the Joe Foss award, which recognized him as one of the best aviators in the Corps. He left the Marine Corps and soon began working with a major inter-national energy company in deepwater and other drilling operations. They had experienced costly trouble with a standard equipment test and needed help. Every two weeks, the company had to conduct routine safety tests on the blowout preventer for each of its active drill pipes. As far as management knew, the tests had been running

---

[5] Ibid.
[6] Ibid.

smoothly until one of the company's best drill operators accidentally sheared the pipe during the test—the drilling equivalent of ejecting from an aircraft. The mistake cost $5 million.

If an experienced driller could make the mistake, the company reasoned that others would, too. So they called Dingee to investigate. He found that the company had in fact had 38 previous close calls in addition to this recent mistake. He also found that the tests had become too routine; workers weren't focused. Even though they'd done the operation hundreds of times, they could still make a mistake. So Dingee and the company scripted the test routine, making sure that every critical action was included in the checklist. The company's drilling tests have remained accident-free ever since checklists were implemented.

"Simplicity can be the biggest barrier to checklists and safey," Dingee says. "It's almost too simple. The world is getting so complex, particularly in oil and gas, that companies expect only shiny, highly complex solutions. They have trouble believing a simple checklist can be transformative and improve execution that much. But it goes back to what we learned in the military: Simplicity combats complexity."

Two factors drive checklist success: the tool itself and the buy-in and follow-through. The right tool will be written correctly and will require someone to engage actively. We're all human. We're naturally lazy and tend to automate functions. Checklists *force* functions and make you be truly conscious. When developing them, find points of natural disengagement and ensure the checklist covers it. Ensure it covers all critical processes. And don't develop them in a vacuum. Engage the people who will be using the checklists. You'll get great information from the frontlines and they'll also readily adopt the checklist system once it's released. A tool can be extraordinary, but if your staff won't use it and your leadership won't support it, it'll be worthless.

Other key characteristics of effective checklists include:

- Support standard operating procedures.
- Remain simple.
- Execute with someone else.
- Include cross-checking.

- Require confirmation other than *yes* or *no*. (What is the flap angle? What is the pressure?)
- Provide a buffer zone for safety.
- Provide for a clear response.
- Have no more than nine steps.

Here's the bottom line: If team members follow checklists, will performance improve and accident rates fall? The answer for big energy companies—and firms in a broad range of industries—has been an emphatic *yes*.

X-GAPS

No matter how hard you work to combat task saturation and its symptoms, every organization still faces a common challenge: humans. Way back in 1885, German psychologist Hermann Ebbinghaus demonstrated that people start forgetting what they've learned as soon as they learn it! His forgetting curve demonstrated that humans forget half of what they learn within an hour of learning it; we forget a full two-thirds by the following day.

The specific processes we've outlined thus far help mitigate our common human weaknesses by giving us simple steps that can ensure successful execution even if we forget some basics. But things will almost always go wrong during execution. We call the difference in planned result and actual result an *execution gap* or *X-gap*. Regular, efficient X-gap meetings help close those holes and improve ongoing execution.

X-gap meetings assume several things:

- Plans and projects are rarely executed as planned.
- In a rapidly-changing environment, plans must be adjusted to keep pace.
- Change, competing demands, and task saturation all interfere with plans.
- Planners often miscalculate or misallocate time and resources.

- Frequent team reviews increase transparency and drive accountability.
- The leader owns responsibility for closing the gap between planning and execution.

Regularly scheduled X-gap meetings keep a project on track by helping a team maintain its execution rhythm despite the bumps, twists, and surprises that will arise. X-gap meetings require that the team come together at predetermined intervals during the execution of a plan or project, address the progress on each individual task, and (if necessary) take action to keep each work stream on track. The regularity of the meetings is critical to sustaining execution rhythm. Regular X-gap meetings maintain accountability and ensure little problems don't snowball into large ones that could throw off the entire project. The meetings will make sure the entire team moves on schedule toward the common goal.

The execution phase relies on accountability—remember, in Step Five of planning, you developed courses of action and assigned *who* does *what, when*. Once a team begins executing, nobody can hide. If you don't perform your assigned duties, others will notice, and ripples from your incomplete tasks may upset the overall project's schedule. The X-gap meeting is a transparent means of applying peer pressure to enhance performance. So watch out for lengthy excuses or tactics people might use to distract the group from individual responsibility. X-gap leaders must keep the meetings productive and on-track.

Leading an effective X-gap meeting requires a commitment to four basic principles:

1. Focus
2. Resolution
3. Action
4. Frequency

Focus: X-Gap meetings should be short and focused only on the tasks at hand. The meeting is not an opportunity for open debate or complex problem solving. Its sole purpose is to review all due and open tasks within a plan. It should be a quick meeting, marked by rapid progress through agenda items. The leader should proceed through the plan and courses of action developed in Step Five task by task, asking each owner for a short progress report. Is the job done or not done? On track or in jeopardy? The meeting's goal is to close execution gaps rhythmically before the gaps get so wide that the mission is compromised. Focus on identifying those tasks that are in jeopardy so the leader and team members can manage them and keep up their execution rhythm. These meetings can be as quick as 5 minutes, but you should aim to keep them under 20.

Resolution: X-gap meetings also aim to resolve uncertainty, ambiguity, or any other obstacles. When a leader identifies an execution gap, he or she needs to fix it. The leader should make decisions and allocate resources to close the gaps. In the meeting itself, the owner of the execution gap should succinctly explain what help is needed. A discussion longer than two minutes is too long. This is not a forum for debate or long-winded excuses. In the military, we're not interested in blaming individuals; we're interested in accomplishing the mission. Sometimes, that's not the prevalent mind-set in civilian business. Part of instilling a culture of high performance comes from shifting the focus to outcomes. How can we work together to achieve this goal? How can we help one another? Team members must realize that blame and anger only hinder the mission.

Remember that we prefer an 80 percent plan now to a 100 percent plan later, when opportunity has already passed us by. X-gap meetings make sure our 80 percent plans stays on track so the debriefing process we discuss in the next chapter can close that remaining 20 percent gap while we move forward. That's a critical part of the resolve component. The courage to execute is, in part, about having a smart bias toward action. You can't wait until everything is perfect; you can adjust and adapt as you go. That is the power of this process—adjusting so the 80 percent plan moves toward 100 percent.

Action: After discussing each task in jeopardy, the leader should have created a list of specific actions to ensure all tasks remain on track. All team members should know if they have a responsibility stemming from the meeting and, if so, exactly what they need to do to manage that responsibility and when they need to do it.

Frequency: Finally, X-gap meetings should be a regular and recognized piece of the execution process. Teams should expect the meeting at the same time and place each week, or at whatever interval you decide is best. This ensures meetings never surprise team members. If they have tasks to accomplish, regular reporting meetings are powerful motivation! X-gap meetings help you keep your execution rhythm.

DEVELOPING LEADERS

"Every Marine a rifleman." That's the saying the Marine Corps uses to describe the core competency of every officer. Every single officer in the corps should be able to execute in the field. They may be a pilot, a logistics officer, or a tank commander, but at their core, they're riflemen. That means they each know how to execute in the thick of combat.

They learn through repetition, in training and in battle. But since they often operate in the tactical realm, on the frontlines, they also practice decentralized decision-making: assessing a situation, evaluating options against the commander's intent, taking action, and adjusting and improvising on the fly. They improve not just through experience, but through an important process of mentorship.

"The U.S. Marine Corps mentorship program is an iterative process," said Major Alex Cross. "Mentees are given tasks and enough room to maneuver to complete them as they see fit. That means they're also given room to make mistakes. But good mentors make sure they learn from them. Failing can be one of the best ways to learn. And when you have a good mentor, he or she can talk you through what went wrong and help you make the right calls next time."

The marine corps mandates that every battalion or squadron have a mentorship program, but true to corps principles, commanders have discretion in implementing it. Good leaders avoid forcing reporting relationships by letting marines find others with similar views or whose advice they value. The corps gives marines the tools and framework to create mentoring relationships; it lets them figure out the details. The mentorship program gives younger marines a channel for giving and getting feedback. They improve and they also help their older mentors improve as well.

This process of mentorship and learning bucks some corps stereotypes. Some people think of marines as rigid, robots who obey orders. In fact, the corps deliberately encourages people to think creatively. Marine leaders are known for their ability to relate to their subordinates, and given that the corps has members from every conceivable background, that takes creativity. They have to give orders and entire teams are relying on subordinates to execute those orders.

"You can say, 'Attack that hill,' and marines will do it, but they can tell when you're giving a bad order," said Cross. "There's a difference between bad orders and unpopular orders. Every day we give unpopular orders. So we have to understand the human dimension behind giving orders. We want people to follow the order and believe it's the right thing to do. That's how we drive great execution. There's an indispensable human dimension to giving orders and leading people. It gets back to creativity and having developed ability through repetition and mentorship."

MISSION CHECKLIST

Brief Your Mission
1. Create a microclimate for success.
   a. Setting
   b. Preparing
   c. Organizing
2. Brief the mission.
   a. B: Brief the scenario.
   b. R: Review the mission objectives.
   c. I: Identify the threats and resources.

(continued)

(*continued*)

    d. E: Execution = courses of action.

    e. F: Flexibility = contingencies.

Execute Your Mission

1. Execution rhythm.
2. X-gap meetings.
3. Manage task saturation.
   a. Utilize checklists.
   b. Utilize cross-checks.
   c. Mutual support/teamwork/task shedding.

CHAPTER 6

CONTINUOUS IMPROVEMENT: THE DEBRIEF IMPERATIVE

Like few other teams, the Blue Angels have made continuous improvement an exact science. They call it debriefing.

The trust that bonds their squadron stems from an absolutely relentless dedication to reviewing their performance, assessing each aviator, and making everyone better. What's particularly notable? Each season, half of this elite-performing team is new—a turnover rate of 50 percent. Yet their meticulous process of debriefing makes them all fly like veterans.

Inside the Blue Angels' hangar at Naval Air Station Pensacola, Florida, is their debriefing room, a veritable shrine to continuous improvement. A fanatical dedication to constant fine-tuning and progress is how this elite, high-performing unit still becomes better each day. After every practice or show, the six Blue Angel pilots gather in the debriefing room, which is an ideal environment for a private and frank discussion. Each team member leaves his rank at the door. During a debrief, no ranks exist. Nothing is personal. Everything is professional. The Blue Angels become a peer group of aviators dedicated to improving the performance of the entire team. They'll never fly the perfect mission, but they aim to get closer every single flight.

They take seats around a long conference table and watch video of their most recent flight on a flat screen monitor. They find the flaws in each part of the mission and discuss them openly. Was Two out of position during the diamond roll maneuver? Did Five roll too late during the inverted-to-inverted pass? The group dissects each maneuver, uncovering the smallest flaws and suggesting solutions in the sole interest of elevating the entire team's performance.

"After a flight, each pilot is afforded the opportunity to admit their own mistakes in front of the team," explained former team member Scott Kartvedt. "This element of debriefing is critical to building trust and confidence within the organization. If an individual can self-admit an error then we believe the individual is more likely to self-correct and self-improve. Once any pilot has admitted their safeties—their execution errors or X-gaps—and their individual debrief is complete, then and only then can another teammate inform that pilot of other execution errors. It takes thick skin to adjust to the self-criticism and even thicker skin to adjust to the corrections from the other pilots. Once every team member recognizes the reason we debrief, the execution and performance of the team improves each and every day." The debrief improves future execution by reinforcing best practices and eliminating execution errors. Debriefs aren't intended to tear someone down. They aspire to build up that individual and create an exceptionally high performer who is reaching his potential and thus helping the squadron as a whole reach its potential.

Entering a debriefing culture is not necessarily easy, however. Kartvedt observed that new aviators join the Blue Angles humble and ready to learn. But after a period of six months, he explained, "We turn back into fighter pilots." Egos begin getting in the way.

During one debrief in Kartvedt's first season, the veteran Number Four pilot, the Blue Angels' training officer, began debriefing him on a particular six-plane delta maneuver. Even though other pilots were also out of position, the training officer focused on Kartvedt, who considered it a personal attack.

That evening at dinner, Kartvedt gave the training officer a cold shoulder; he literally turned his back to him. The veteran had seen this before. He turned Kartvedt around and said, "Hey, this isn't personal; this is professional. I know you can be better tomorrow and you can fix the mistakes you made today."

Kartvedt realized that Number Four was telling him that he believed in him, not that he doubted him. The veteran believed Kartvedt could do better and he finally understood that debriefing is supportive, not adversarial. Only through individual and team accountability—and willingness to take and use criticism—can the Blue Angels claim to be the best in the world.

The most important thing teams do when they take action may be what they do immediately after they execute the plan: *debrief*, the fourth and final stage of the Flawless Execution engine. The debrief is often the most overlooked and underutilized part of the engine, especially in business. Too many corporate teams plan, brief, and execute, then they go right back to planning! Plan, brief, execute; plan, brief, execute. That's a shame because those teams are missing a tremendous opportunity to improve with every cycle and increase their future effectiveness.

Admiral Ron Horton saw debriefing work at every level of the USS *Enterprise* when he was captain. In particular, he saw it almost eliminate flight deck crunches, collisions with or between planes. With nearly 100 aircraft aboard ship and hundreds of men on the flight and hangar decks, collisions seem inevitable. On one cruise, a misinterpreted hand signal led to a sailor raising the jet blast deflector at the wrong time, knocking the wing off a waiting jet. On another, a maintainer removed wheel chocks early and one aircraft rolled into another. Tow trucks traveling too fast have collided with planes, aircraft have pivoted into one another, and elevator guardrails have snagged landing gear. In 100 years of carrier aviation, flight decks have seen every mistake imaginable. So many opportunities exist for mistakes that it seems impossible to eliminate them, but aboard *Enterprise*, under Horton's command, debriefing did.

After every series of flight operations, flight deck crews would debrief. They reviewed anything that had the potential to compromise their mission objective. Was the plane captain where he was supposed to be to ensure safety? Was the wing-walker checking the wingsweep to make sure no planes were within the radius? Were aircraft turned at the right points? If tow trucks were driving too fast, the debrief would uncover the reason and the team would fix the problem. Perhaps there was a communication error that nearly caused an accident; were standard operating procedures violated? Do the men need more training? Does a process need adjustment?

"We didn't care who made the mistake," explained then-captain Horton. "Our philosophy is that if *that* guy made the mistake, there are 50 other people who made the mistake, or who could. We want to prevent the mistake, not punish the person. We're not going to fire or crucify anyone. Things will happen. People will make mistakes, but we want to learn from them. It's easy to shoot the operator when in fact you probably have procedure issues, communication issues, or training issues. Why did that guy do what he did? I can *guarantee* it wasn't because he came in that morning and said, 'I'm going to screw this up.' Debriefs are nameless and rankless and they help you be a better team. On *Enterprise*, they saved taxpayers a lot of money. On that cruise we had maybe $100 in flight deck damage. That's extraordinary."

The same principles were adopted by Medtronic, the inventor of the pacemaker and one of America's largest medical device manufacturers. The company's heart valve division had been struggling for five years. Employees were often transferred to the ailing department as a prelude to retirement or as a consequence of underperformance. It was plagued by quality issues and morale issues; its largest competitor had become dominant. Experienced executive Rick Carrion took over the division to revive it. Using Flawless Execution principles, he instilled a new level of accountability in the organization, during both planning and execution.

Using the our six-step planning process, Carrion's team assigned clear responsibilities; every action had an owner, a person's name beside it. Then during quarterly debriefings, everyone was held accountable. Did they do what they said they would? If not, why? How could the team help? As the Medtronic heart valve division began debriefing, they identified what was and wasn't working; people had no place to hide. There were no excuses, only results and solutions.

Carrion observed, "Planning and debriefing enforces a disciplined process. Either you did or you didn't do what you said you would. It injects a new level of accountability and low performers don't like it. They'll self-select to leave. High performers thrive in a debriefing system, however. It provides a forum for talking about their success and those lessons lift up the entire team."

The process was particularly enlightening for Carrion as a leader. He explained that debriefing can completely change the culture of an organization; in fact, he considers debriefing a culture, not an event. "As a leader, it was hard for me to stand up and list the mistakes I made—and what I was going to do about them," he said. "You have to accept that to create a culture of accountability, you can always do something better. You have to leave your ego at the door, create a safe environment for everyone, and be sincere. The moment you admit you made a mistake, it empowers everyone in the room. Your team will start improving quarter after quarter, year after year. You absolutely cannot get mad at someone in the debrief!"[1]

As the team embraced this new mindset, its confidence returned and its performance increased. Medtronic began reclaiming market share. Several months later, the team poached their dominant competitor's largest client. Within three years, they had regained market leadership. In the complexity of the medical device market, Medtronic used a simple process to turn around an entire division. The value of simplicity and the debriefing process isn't confined to business and military teams only. It can apply anywhere, to anyone.

At their first bye week in the 2011–2012 season, the New York Giants had a four-and-two record, but believed they weren't executing in line with their considerable talent. Coach Tom Coughlin and quarterback Eli Manning wanted another trip to the Super Bowl, which they'd won in 2008. To have a chance at reaching the NFL championship game in Indianapolis, the team needed to improve its execution on the field by improving communication off the field. They adopted the nameless, rankless debrief.

The players and the players' leadership council decided to allocate 30 minutes of their own time after each remaining game to discuss what went well and what didn't. No coaches were allowed; it was all players. And since the collective bargaining agreement limited their practice time, the players were, in fact, donating their own time for the player-only debriefs. The debriefing process wasn't always easy to implement. When ranks came off and a safe environment was created, some long-held frustration came out. Players let fly with gripes that had been nagging them for months, and in the first debriefs, some of the team's units underwent a true catharsis; they got burdens off their chests and forced issues into the open where they could finally be resolved.

Eli Manning and Justin Tuck led debriefs for the offense and defense, respectively. "I wasn't coaching anybody," said Manning. "I was just coaching myself, looking at what I needed to do better

---

[1]Rick Carrion. Interview with the author, August 10, 2013.

and telling everybody. Then everybody would talk about what they needed to do to improve."

"It wasn't about calling people out," elaborated Giants linebacker Mathias Kiwanuka. "It was an opportunity to see everybody hold themselves accountable."[2]

As the continuous improvement process took root over the remainder of the season, players on offense and defense became exceptional debriefers. They would volunteer their own mistakes and explain how they'd improve next week. Sometimes they'd ask for assistance, or point to where another player could help them prepare or execute a play. The season progressed through the winter and the nameless, rankless debriefs continued to improve the team's performance. In January 2012, the Giants won the 2011–2012 NFC Championship. Two weeks later, they won Super Bowl XLVI.

The next season, Afterburner teams of former military professionals taught the Green Bay Packers, Washington Redskins, and Denver Broncos how to debrief. It was validating to hear announcers comment on Peyton Manning's new practice of debriefing his offense after each series. Peyton was working hard to get inside the execution cycle of his brother Eli because he knew the team with the shortest and most effective Flawless Execution cycle wins.

Marine corps major general John Admire understood Peyton Manning's strategy. The general said, "If your decision-making loop is more streamlined than your enemy's, then you set the pace and course of the battle."[3] Whoever can design plays, huddle, make plays, and adjust the fastest will win. How efficiently can you *plan, brief, execute, and debrief?*

When used diligently and strategically, debriefing powers a continuous improvement engine that can elevate the performance of any team, no matter how elite it may already be. The Giants had won the 2008 Super Bowl. They were a great team. But they knew they

---

[2]Damon Hack, "One Giant Leap for Manningkind," *Sports illustrated*, February 13, 2012, 44.

[3]David H. Freedman. "Corps Values," Inc., April 4, 1998. www.inc.com/maga zine/19980401/906.html.

competed in a cutthroat and ever-improving NFL, so to win the Super Bowl again in 2012, they had to continue improving incrementally, every single week.

THE STEALTH DEBRIEF

Organizations that don't debrief often equate failure with retribution or negative consequences. An NFL team without a debriefing culture might see a missed tackle or blown coverage as a failure. A team *with* a debriefing culture will see it as an opportunity to improve and to understand if something systemic might have caused the error. Blaming the linebacker or defensive back and stopping there would leave the root cause unaddressed. Perhaps coaching or training led to the mistake, and if that goes uncorrected other players will continue making the same mistakes. Debriefers see mistakes and failures as golden opportunities—and the sooner they surface the better. If you're a military aviator or special operator, you can't afford to make the same mistake twice. If you do, you may not come home.

In debriefing, patience and genuine commitment to the team's mission are vital traits. The debriefer has to keep the team's good in mind and remember that the debrief isn't about punishing or rewarding someone. After one flight where a training instructor gave a failing grade to a young ensign, she spent the entire afternoon debriefing him, not simply discussing what went right or wrong on that mission, but helping him learn how to do better next time.

"I helped him with how to study and how to chair-fly the mission," said flight instructor Amber Dempsen. "We went over the mission then chair-flew it again together, sitting in our chairs and doing the entire flight. I really wanted to help him succeed, so we spent a lot of time on it.

"That's why we had such a long debrief. He just needed to spend more time on it and, hopefully, he learned that he'll always need to spend that much time preparing for a flight. It's serious business."

I spent long hours chair-flying myself, before and after missions. It was my prep and my debrief. It's part of that military process that gave me the courage to step into a single-seat fighter jet and go execute. When I was first becoming a pilot, I felt a bit chastened every time an instructor would chair-fly a mission with me. I felt like a grade-schooler being reprimanded. But I soon realized that: (1) great pilots aren't simply born, and (2) the instructor cared less about the mistakes and far more about making me a great pilot. I hope my instructor liked me, but that's not relevant to why he spent time debriefing me. He or she did it so I'd perform well for the air force one day; so I'd achieve my mission goals and keep everyone around me safe. Debriefing is the essence of teamwork.

To create an atmosphere conducive to civil and effective debriefing, like that created in training squadrons, the New York Giants and Denver Broncos used our process known as STEALTH to conduct their nameless, rankless debriefs. The acronym stands for:

Set the time

Tone

Execution versus objectives

Analyze execution

Lessons learned

Transfer lessons learned

High note

Here they are, one by one.

Set the time: Establish specific times and places for debriefing during mission planning. And don't forget to set end times; people don't look forward to meetings that won't end on time. When I'd return from a mission—successful or not—I'd go into my debrief exactly 45 minutes after I landed; that's standard operating procedure. When I arrived, I'd have my onboard radar and HUD videos cued and my notes would be ready. To the extent I could, I'd have already identified my mistakes. I'd get to the debriefing room, close the door, and my flight lead and I would meet for a specified period of time to debrief.

Then I'd take the lessons and improve. It's the idea then-captain Mewbourne expressed aboard *Eisenhower*: "Better each day."

Before the debrief, make sure everyone knows what's expected and what to expect. When I walked into the room, I expected three things: First, that the room would be prepped. Second, that we'd start on time. Third, that we'd end on time. This wouldn't drag into an endless postmortem. Basically, all participants need to know these five items:

1. **Time**. The debrief needs a specified beginning time and end time, and since the STEALTH debrief has seven components, each needs its own time slot.

2. **Location**. We talked about creating a microclimate for success in the briefing process, and the debrief is no different. Make sure to pick a room that allows you to concentrate. In my squadron, we had one room designated for debriefing. Everyone knew that when you walked into that room, it was time to be serious, and leave your rank and ego at the door.

3. **Participants**. Identify and include the people who *need* to be present—and no one else. You'll want to have the personnel who are directly involved with the mission or project, but extra bodies or opinions can distract from the focus and openness a good debrief should create. Supervisors and bosses who were not part of the execution may compromise that vital nameless/rankless environment.

4. **Roles**. Whether military or civilian, every debrief needs a leader, a timekeeper, a scribe, and a data input designate. The leader is usually the same person who led the brief for the mission, and he or she is often not the highest-ranking person in the room. The leader is the person held accountable for the overall success of the mission. Debriefs can become interminably long and drawn-out affairs without a good timekeeper. Our goal is to review the mission and identify lessons efficiently. Identify what went right, what went wrong, and why. You'll worry about the details and solutions later. In the debrief, you just want to capture the facts, and you should do that as

quickly as possible. If you're using whiteboards, make sure you have a designated scribe with legible handwriting! Regardless of how you're recording the information, make sure someone owns that responsibility. Someone also needs to collect, input, analyze, finalize, and disseminate the debrief data.

5. **Future steps**. Everyone should leave the debrief understanding what went well and what didn't, and who owns the solution. At the beginning, make sure you've clearly defined the objectives for the debrief. Then as you identify execution gaps, assign a single point of accountability for finding a solution. But don't try to find the solution *during* the debrief. That comes later.

<u>Tone</u>: When the Blue Angels or the Thunderbirds sit down to debrief, nobody outranks anyone else. A lieutenant can point out mistakes made by a colonel. Nor does anyone use real names. They refer to Number One or Number Two, not Scott or Frank. The debrief isn't personal; it's high-stakes business. In some squadrons, pilots will literally rip their Velcro ranks and nametags off their uniform. Going rankless creates an environment where:

- Nobody fears reprimand for pointing out errors, whether their own or those of someone else.
- Observations are fact-based, not opinion-based.
- The goal is group improvement, not personal reputation building.
- Only one person speaks at a time.

Participants aren't interested in ranks or personalities; they're interested in improving their team's level of execution. And those egos? We leave them at the door as well. So every debrief should be nameless and rankless in order to facilitate open communication. Responsibility for setting that tone falls to the leader. The leader should first openly admit his or her errors and ask for feedback from team members; this will set the tone for the entire debrief and inspire open communication. It's all in the third person, and it's not *who's* right, but *what's* right.

I always suggest that leaders start the debrief by offering two or three ways they could have performed better, then ask others for two or three instances where they think the leader could have done better. The purpose of the exercise isn't to turn yourself into a punching bag; rather, you're establishing the tone and showing you're vested in this nameless, rankless process.

I've also seen businesses place artificial harmony over truth. They'll sweep mistakes or successes under the table so everyone feels good; nobody gets hurt feelings. This is the *worst* thing you can do for your execution. If you shy away from addressing the issues a debrief uncovers, you're wasting everyone's time. Artificial harmony helps nobody except your competitors. If you don't address root problems, I can assure you they'll fester and surface sooner or later. By debriefing and addressing them as soon as possible, you can proactively manage their effects and improve your organization.

Execution versus objectives: Quite simply, did your execution achieve your objectives? Did you meet the mission objective, and did you adhere to the course of action? You can't debrief against an objective that's not clear and measurable. If the team didn't understand the mission objective, you may have done a poor job in the brief. In fact, a good debrief leader first asks if the team understood the mission objective. If they didn't, that's issue number one.

Analyze execution: What were the results? Why did your team achieve its goals? Or why not? What were the causes and root causes of failure? This is where we look at the errors and successes and ask, "Why?" Then we ask *why* again and again until we peel back the layers of a result or action and determine what truly caused it. You're looking for three things:

1. Results
2. *How* you got the results
3. *Why* you got the results

Results are easy enough to see—as long as you planned effective measures. The first "why" you ask often leads to how something happened. That's often active human error. But through experience, I can guarantee your answer to that first-level *why* won't lead you to the underlying cause. Why was that human error committed? You must look deeper and I never consider stopping until I've asked *why* at least four times. Like Admiral Horton said, nobody ever shows up for work planning to screw up. You have to look deeper to uncover the why. We'll talk more about this when we discuss root cause analysis.

Lessons learned: To improve future planning and results, and to build organizational knowledge, develop a list of lessons learned. These lessons should be ones that are actionable so your team can easily use them to improve performance on its next project.

Transfer lessons learned: Don't just keep lessons learned inside your team; share them with the organization. If you found an error, design a checklist, a message, or some other tool to prevent the same mistake from happening again. Use the debrief to accelerate future performance by communicating the lessons to your entire organization. Again, if you don't leverage the debrief, you're wasting time.

The United States Marine Corps Center for Lessons Learned (MCCLL) manages the invaluable lessons coming from marine after action reports and debriefs. It supports the Marine Corps Vision & Strategy 2025, which states, "Amid the high risk and uncertainty of combat, shared experience—especially lessons hard-learned—should be promulgated laterally as quickly as possible so that the learning curve of the entire organization is elevated by the creativity or misfortune of the individual units." I'd argue business strategies should include the same type of statement. The trick for most companies, however, becomes capturing the data first, then distributing it so people can use it.

To make sure marines have access to these lessons, the Center supports an expansive database and publishes a monthly newsletter that proactively shares findings with its readers. Its personnel conduct interviews and debriefs with subjects in target areas, like security teams returning from joint duty with Afghan forces. In that instance, lessons learned centered on the necessity of leveraging interpersonal skills in situations where U.S. officers do not have authority over Afghan security details. The next marine units to deploy for security duty will arrive with this and other lessons already in mind. The lessons learned feed into that plan-brief-execute-debrief engine that we believe defines effective execution in any organization. Imagine if most American business planners had access to a database they could search for lessons to apply to their next strategic initiative or tactical mission. Imagine if they simply used the debrief process.

High note: Never end on a negative. Even if the project or task you're debriefing went badly, find the silver lining. Even in failure, positive lessons abound. Focus on things that will help your team improve, and that will help them embrace a culture of debriefing. Only when teams see the positive benefits and uplifting perspective of debriefing will they fully invest themselves in the process and culture. Again, never end on a negative. Your team must understand that debriefing is as much about perpetuating success and understanding why things go well as it is about preventing issues. Hopefully you'll spend more time doing root-cause analysis around successes than around errors.

ROOT-CAUSE ANALYSIS

Let's discuss root-cause analysis, which has four key components: core, planning, team, and execution. Within each category, you'll see a set of terms, many of which you've seen earlier. Why? Effective organizations share a common language.

Common language is vital to assembling a high-performing team. In the military, I learned more acronyms and jargon than I thought could exist, but everyone else had learned the same language and we could communicate quickly and effectively. Observations and orders weren't lost in translation. When we plan and debrief, that common language is essential. Particularly when we debrief at all levels of an organization, we need standard categories.

Core

Foremost within the core category is the basic element of any team or organization: people. Bringing the right people onboard and training (or indoctrinating) them effectively will determine your success.

Great product but a bad sales team? You'll be out of business. Great product, great sales team, but back office staff whose values aren't aligned? Watch out. When people are identified as an issue's root cause, you have to dig a bit deeper. If we identified a problem with one of my squadron's engine maintainers, we didn't just focus on his or her actions. It's *possible* that he or she just decided to underperform one day, but that was highly unlikely. We looked deeper for the systemic problems. Perhaps the maintainer didn't understand the instructions or goal; perhaps training was inadequate.

In fact, training is often a root cause. Effective organizations must have people who are trained to act appropriately. In a complex military environment, years of training and practice are often needed for a soldier or sailor or officer to develop the skills necessary to execute his or her role flawlessly. Elite military teams know how to train people rapidly, as the time value of action demands. They also know the danger of inadequate or improper training. Some things aren't worth sacrificing for expediency.

Another flaw in the people equation is often rooted in the hiring or placement process. Maybe we were hiring the wrong types of people for the job. In root-cause analysis, we're trying to get to the *root cause*, not just place blame on the *most proximate* cause. Unit or corporate standards for hiring, training, performance, or behavior all drive individual actions, so we were always making sure our squadron standards provided the baseline for success.

Another core root cause may be strategy. Maybe a mission failed because we fell short in designing our strategy. Did we identify the right critical leverage points? Were our plans based on good situational awareness? It's possible we had a great strategy at the beginning of a battle, but when the enemy suddenly reveals it has three active fighter squadrons in the area, it's time to adjust. In today's world, battlefields change rapidly and can quickly render a strategy ineffective, but that's expected. As a business, you just need to pivot quickly and adjust your strategy when new technology emerges, consumer tastes suddenly shift, or competitors drop prices.

Core-category root cause could also go beyond strategy to the high-definition destination and how well the leader's intent cascaded through the organization. If a field commander destroyed an enemy's power plant in the process of taking it out, did that align with the military's planned future state for the battlespace? Maybe, as was the case in Iraq, the military wanted to preserve the infrastructure to facilitate rebuilding after the hostile regime toppled. A commander may have called in artillery on the power plant (the proximate cause of mission failure), but the root cause was that he or she didn't understand the high-definition destination (HDD) clearly enough. The debrief process is not a blame game. The process aims to find what went wrong or well and why, then determine how to fix the mistakes or repeat the successes next time.

Planning

Were there specific flaws in the six-step planning process? Were the objectives clear, measurable, achievable, and aligned with your HDD? The best teams in the world will still fall short of their goals if they're following flawed plans. Let's say U.S. Central Command (CENTCOM) sends a Ranger unit on a prisoner exfiltration and assigns a squadron for air support. During planning, the team identified the troops and terrain around the prisoners of war (POWs) as key threats. A fighter escort could neutralize the two attack helicopters the enemy also had at the target. But what if planners failed to identify the enemy air base 100 miles away as a threat? The fighter escort may down the defending helicopters and the team may land safely, but how many fighters are scrambling from the air base nearby? How many will be overhead when our helicopters are ready to extract the Rangers and their rescued POWs? If planners miss a threat, the mission can implode. Identifying threats as well as available resources is just good risk management. Root-cause analysis seeks to find holes in risk management, places where we should have seen threats, but didn't. Did we plan with a realistic understanding of the possible threats and the resources we had to offset them? If not, why?

As the root-cause analysis process continues assessing the six steps of planning, it reviews if planners used lessons already learned by other teams. It explores whether courses of action included *who* will do *what* and *when*. Were red teams brought in to improve the plan? Were contingency plans in place with clear triggers? Identifying a threat is half the battle; managing the threat wins the battle. Effective threat management demands a well-developed contingency plan. If an extra squadron of enemy aircraft arrive on scene, do we have enough fighters on standby to cover the Rangers' extraction? Oversights in all these areas of planning can lead to mission failures. Identifying and addressing them during the debrief process will prevent the same mistakes in the future. In combat, that saves lives. In the NFL, it saves wins. In business, it saves profit.

Team

We always say individual execution is one thing, but organizational execution is everything, and you can't execute at 100 percent if your team isn't aligned or doesn't exhibit those key traits that mark effective teams. Having studied teams in business and the military, we've identified six qualities that enable a team's success. Without those traits, you're going to have a tough road. The traits are:

1. Leadership
2. Organization
3. Communication
4. Knowledge
5. Experience
6. Discipline

Again, military personnel love to use acronyms, so we call this LOCKED. I'll revisit these principles in a later chapter, but it's important to diagnose a failure with these traits in mind. A team with poor leadership, misaligned organization, poor communication, inadequate knowledge, little experience, or poor discipline will not execute at the level needed to achieve difficult objectives. In a static, low-stakes environment, sure, you might still meet success if your team lacks some of these traits, but elite military teams don't operate in that type of lax environment—and I'd bet you don't, either.

Execution

Crosschecks, mutual support, checklists, and task shedding all combat task saturation, which can pose the biggest threat to flawless execution. Your training, planning, and briefing are for naught if your team members get task saturated. In early aviation, pilots had far fewer complications and threats to manage than they do today. They didn't have to fly crowded approach patterns, manage radio communications, or worry about myriad cockpit instruments or variables. Many times, their accidents were attributed to mechanical malfunctions or simple pilot errors in navigation or aircraft control. Then aircraft started becoming more complex machines. The advent of good radio communication added another scoop of duties to an aviator's plate, and as aviation proliferated, rules and patterns were imposed on formerly open air space. Pilots' plates were getting full. Mishap investigators began noticing good pilots making preventable mistakes because they weren't managing the increasing complexity of their jobs. Good pilots were simply becoming too distracted or overwhelmed. In time, this phenomenon became known as task saturation.

Today, when the military delves into root-cause analysis of an accident or a mission, task saturation often surfaces as the culprit, but that alone is not entirely helpful. What's more telling is uncovering why the pilot failed to fight off task saturation. Which of the methods failed him? Did he or she fail to use cross-checks and forget to monitor the attitude indicator? Did a wingman not help an overwhelmed pilot shed low-priority tasks, or did the pilot fail to use checklists? Answering these questions gets to the root cause of mission failures and provides information a squadron or company can use to improve future missions.

Root-Cause Identification Matrix

Core	Planning	Team	Execution
People Hiring practices and screening; employment policy; sufficient external labor resources	**Objective** Clear, measurable, achievable, and aligned	**Leadership** Leader holds self and team accountable, models appropriate behaviors, and enforces standards	**Task Saturation** Too much to do and too little time to do it; mitigated by the practices below
Training Knowledge and skills that should exist given known or anticipated needs	**Threats** Risks assessed to include known threats and "known unknown" threats	**Organization** Physical organization of things; unambiguous roles and responsibilities; organization and coordination of meetings	**Cross-Checks —Priorities** Prioritize and execute to the highest priorities first, particularly when task saturated
Standards Defined processes, instructions, guidance, or doctrine	**Resources** Available resources identified to negate, mitigate, or avoid threats; additional needed resources identified	**Communication** Brief plans; maintain clear expectations and alignment between individual activity, strategy and HDD; maintain Situational Awareness^{SM}	**Mutual Support** Team members support and value each other; take responsibility to point out "dumb, different, and dangerous"; aid others who are task saturated.

Root-Cause Identification Matrix (*continued*)

Core	Planning	Team	Execution
Strategy Plan is clear, measurable, achievable, and supports the HDD	**Lessons Learned** Draw upon experience of team/entire organization and lessons-learned databases to improve plan	**Knowledge** Collaborate and include cognitive diversity on the team; seek the best information available	**Checklists** Use wherever appropriate; utilize course of action as a checklist
HDD Clear, simple, believable, and detailed	**Course of Action** Clear, written course of action with "who, what, and when"; Reviewed through red-teaming	**Experience** Include both novices and experts on team; debrief to accelerate experience	**X-gap** Short, focused team meetings to analyze execution to date and close execution gaps
	Contingencies Planned response to threats with clear triggers	**Discipline** Adherence to standards and plans	

Here's another example. NASA's two X-31 experimental jets had logged nearly 500 successful test flights by the mid 1990s. Aircraft Number One was testing its automatic control system during its 292nd flight. The test failed, however. As the aircraft returned to base, something went very wrong. The pilot saw conflicting airspeeds on his gauges then the plane began porpoising out of control. With all control gone, the pilot ejected and more than $50 million in machinery and electronics crashed to the ground. So, what happened?

NASA had replaced a heated sensor with an unheated one that could not ward off ice. To counteract any negative effects, the standard operating procedures for the flight specified that the pilot not fly near visible moisture, like clouds. But he did anyway. Since the sensor was unheated, vapor settled on it and froze. The accumulated ice prevented the sensor from correctly registering air pressure and airspeed, which sent the plane out of control. The pilot and ground crew were not aware of, or did not exercise, a manual override that would have allowed the pilot to regain control of the aircraft.

What were the causes of the accident? First, the pilot violated standard operating procedure by flying near moisture. He assumed he could mitigate the risk of water vapor freezing by using the heated probe to ward off any ice. Had the probe been heated, he might have been correct, but it wasn't. The incident's related cause statement might read: "Moisture noted but not deemed serious risk."

The pilot did not deem moisture a critical risk because he was not briefed accordingly. The second cause statement could read: "Pilot did not know probe was unheated."

When the automatic control system test failed earlier in the flight, pilot and crew should have known something was amiss, since the test relied on the same sensors whose failure led to the crash. The third and fourth cause statements could read: "Airspeed input incorrect due to frozen probe," and "Team failed to note potential threat to mission."

The final cause of the accident was the pilot's failure to override the automatic control system, which he could have done had he known the right procedures. Instead, he ejected.

Okay, but what was at the root of the crash? What drove the actions or inactions that led to these causes?

First, the pilot flew near the visible moisture without full knowledge: root cause number one. He wasn't aware that the probe was unheated because he wasn't properly briefed. Secondly, even though he thought he could mitigate risks, he still violated standard operating procedures by flying near clouds and vapor. That decision showed a lack of discipline and adherence to standards: root causes number two and three. You also might say the mission team failed to plan for likely contingencies such as moisture. The team should have preplanned to fly around any clouds that appeared. Flying near moisture violated a key rule, which left no room for errors in other systems. If my experience in cockpits taught me anything, it taught me that if something can go wrong, it often will. (My last name, after all, is Murphy, like the thorny law.) Never leave yourself without a margin for error or malfunction. Root cause number four could be inadequate planning.

Some of the same root causes pop up when we look across the proximate causes we identified. We see a consistent gap in knowledge, communication, and standards. I call those recurring root causes and that's where I'd focus my energy. Fixing those will get me 80 percent of the way there.

By looking at these root causes, we see underlying issues that are organizational in nature. We don't get distracted by what the pilot did or did not do. We see *why*. In the legal world, root cause analysis often uncovers the deeper systemic issues that can lead to serious liability. Rarely does any single actor bear the entire blame.

MISSION CHECKLIST

Debrief Your Mission
1. S: Set time and place.
2. T: Tone (nameless and rankless).
3. E: Execution versus objectives.
4. A: Analyze execution.
   a. Result
   b. Cause
   c. Root cause

(continued)

(*continued*)

5. L: Lessons learned.
    a. Lesson learned
    b. Single point of accountability
    c. Timeline
6. T: Transfer lessons learned.
7. H: High note.

CHAPTER 7

LEADERSHIP ON PURPOSE: DEVELOPING TEAMS AND LEADERS FROM DAY ONE

Earlier, we said that individual execution is one thing, organizational execution is everything. That's supremely important in the armed forces because the military executes as a team, often as a team of teams, but we don't think of the army or navy or air force as a team itself, at least in the true sense. Teams are defined by the personal working relationships between members. If I can't name everyone in a group, I don't consider it a team. Size matters here. A small cohesive group can act like a team. An entire 50-person sales force may call itself a team, but it most likely functions like an organization. Show me a 10-person industry group within that larger organization, however, and I might be able to show you a real team. It's about being able to communicate and work together effectively.

It's also about moving toward a common goal, the other defining trait of a real team. At the highest level, a senior leadership team is responsible for leading the organization to the high-definition destination (HDD), that overarching yet highly detailed future with a two-to-five-year time horizon. Strategic objectives reside at the next level, in the form of goal markers. Divisions and other sub-groups aspire to achieve these targets over 6, 12, or 24 months. Tactical mission objectives are at the operational level, and frontline teams are out there in the field striving to achieve them. Those objectives usually come with timeframes of 30, 60, or 90 days. At every level of an organization, at any given moment, a team is working to plan and reach a destination or objective.

What qualities mark a high-performing team? We've identified six that we call LOCKED, since when fighter pilots are locked onto a target, they'll get it. Likewise, teams with these six characteristics are able to achieve their goals.

1. **L**eadership—develops, aligns, and holds the team accountable.
2. **O**rganization—defines roles, processes, and documents.
3. **C**ommunication—enables information sharing and coordination.
4. **K**nowledge—concerns acquiring, identifying, and utilizing information.

5. **E**xperience—provides know-how needed for success.
6. **D**iscipline—keeps the team focused on the right things.

LEADERSHIP

Leadership comes first because it affects all other aspects of a high-performing team. You can have the other five characteristics in spades, but poor leadership can doom any team. Everyone has seen what poor leadership does to teams in business, sports, healthcare, or education, and we've unfortunately seen examples of that in the military, just like in any other organization. But in the armed forces, we've also seen some of the finest leaders in the world and have identified the qualities of leadership that create elite teams that achieve their objectives.

A good leader ensures that their team owns success, but, at least outwardly, the leader owns the failure. That means being smart about taking responsibility. You must hold yourself accountable for the team's ultimate performance, but do all in your power to help everyone succeed. If you see someone floundering, step in and help. It's your job to clear the way and empower the team to achieve its goals, including supporting accountability. When you reach those goals, just remember a *team* got you there. If you don't make your goal, shoulder the blame appropriately and capture the lessons learned.

Nothing can render a leader irrelevant as fast as hypocrisy. If a leader asks one thing of a team but does the opposite himself, he or she will lose all legitimacy. When that happens, people just won't take their leaders seriously or follow them anywhere. Likewise, leaders must follow and reinforce the organization's standards and processes. Very few leaders, even CEOs, agree with 100 percent of an organization's operating procedures, but good leaders know they must follow all of them and demand that their people do the same. If leaders become selective about the policies they follow, their teams will adopt the same attitude, not only toward corporate policies and decisions, but toward team decisions and procedures as well.

In the military, standards are particularly important because they give every member of the organization a measurement of quality, a common understanding of process, and a reference point for when they are operating at or beyond the envelope—when they are seizing new opportunities in unfamiliar areas. We don't want to stifle innovation or slow down a mission because our people are unsure how to act vis-à-vis our standards and policies. We want those to be crystal clear in their definition and inviolability. Our people need to know the parameters—what they can and cannot do. Beyond that, we'll trust them to improvise and be creative.

Particularly as teams act in fast-changing or new environments, they must maintain situational awareness. And this is the leader's responsibility. The team needs to know the reality of the situation. If Green Beret leaders aren't cultivating situational awareness (SA) during a mission, execution will get sloppy and dangerous. Teams in hostile territory cannot afford to stop tracking their surroundings, and all those things that could impact their ability to achieve their mission objective. In an urban mission, for example, teams will need to track each other, their distance from support, the positions of bystanders and civilians, the time, and the enemy. Business teams must likewise focus on tracking their products, clients or customers, other teams and departments within the company, the market environment, suppliers, regulators, new technologies, and competitors. Lose SA and you lose your objective. Lose sight, lose the fight. Leaders can't let that happen.

Effective leaders don't just issue orders. They listen, actively and carefully. When bullets are flying, it's easy to hear a report and dismiss it, or plan to consider it later. You're leading a unit taking fire from 50 bad guys and you don't have time to listen to a young lieutenant's ideas to flank them, but if you listened actively, over the din of the firefight, you might find your key to victory. Active listening is equally important when businesses are locked in cutthroat competition. We can become so focused on the urgent that we lose ability to think creatively and attack problems from new directions. Take time to listen to them, and your people will surprise you with their good ideas.

Facilitating and delegating are two other critical components of effective leadership. Leaders should seek opportunities to delegate authority to accomplish tasks, and even plan and execute missions, to their subordinates. Most people need some autonomy. They need to succeed or fail on their own merits. That's how they develop as team members and leaders themselves. When leaders can empower others to own a work stream or product, trust is created, individuals are more vested, and the entire team should see better results.

Alexandre Dumas's musketeers often said, "All for one, and one for all." That adage has held true for elite warriors fighting with swords, flintlocks, and M-16s. Great teams support each other, and great leaders must orchestrate that mutual support among team members to ensure each individual is vested in the success of the others. Mutual support means that every member of the team supports the group as a whole as it works toward a common goal. Leaders of high-performing teams encourage their people to ask these two questions. First, *is there someone on my team that needs my help in achieving our objective?* Second, *do I need help from someone on my team to achieve our objective?*

But perhaps most important—and underlying all else—is the idea of integrity. Do you do what you say you'll do? Do you exhibit those values you lift up, that you tell others to embrace? Entire books are written about integrity, but it really boils down to those two questions. If your team trusts you to follow through on your promises and if they see you walking your own talk, they'll follow you just about anywhere.

Checklist: Good Team Leaders
- Take responsibility: A team owns success; a leader owns failure.
- Enforce accountability for themselves and their team members.
- Model an appropriate example.
- Reinforce standards and processes.
- Cultivate situational awareness.
- Listen actively.
- Facilitate collaboration.
- Delegate, trust, and develop leadership in others.
- Orchestrate mutual support.
- Thank and reward team members.

ORGANIZATION

A team leader can use the leadership checklist above to ensure he or she is creating a positive team environment on a daily basis. While everyone on a team should display some elements of leadership, ultimate responsibility rests on one person. The other components of the LOCKED model, however, deal with entire teams and organizational execution. First comes organization itself. Organization includes the way teams align their members to get things done. Part of that is physical. Are you a platoon with two key leaders? Are you a large, diverse business unit, organized by industry? Or are you like America's 2008 Ryder Cup team, sorted into like-minded pods?

Another aspect of organization relates to the roles, standards, and common processes that must be present to achieve a level of high performance. Believe me, no organization has more standard operating procedures than the U.S. military. We have standards for just about everything. In the aviation community, those standards are often written in blood. They exist because people have died. Even when we find them cumbersome or irritating, we always pay attention to the rules. We know there is a reason behind them, so when we're planning or executing missions, we always consider what team or organization activities are already governed by documented standards and processes. Those standards and processes define our organization.

As active military professionals, we participated in, observed, and distilled the cycle of planning, briefing, executing, and debriefing that we call the Flawless Execution engine. Organizing for high levels of team execution requires clear measurements, defined roles, clearly stated courses of action, and contingency plans with unambiguous triggers. Without these essential organizing tools, team execution will suffer.

By using the Flawless Execution engine, organizations create *execution rhythm* or *battle rhythm*, that cyclical set of intentional, periodic leadership intersection points where planning, communication, and assessment activities occur to align execution and close execution gaps (X-gaps).

Teams must organize to support good execution rhythm, which is a powerfully churning cycle of *plan, brief, execute, debrief*. Embedded in that structure should be clear courses of action and X-gap meetings, those short, focused, regular meetings by teams where the tasks within a course of action are reviewed for progress, and steps are taken to close gaps and adapt to changing circumstances. In effect, courses of action are checklists and X-gap meetings are the disciplined process of reviewing the team's progress according to those checklists. So in X-gap meetings, and everywhere else, effective teams organize themselves with checklists. They're simple, but outrageously effective in combating task saturation.

High-performing organizations:

- Refer and adhere to organizational standards and processes.
- Establish clear measurements.
- Define roles.
- Set clear courses of action.
- Plan for contingencies with unambiguous triggers.
- Establish and adhere to execution rhythm.
- Perform X-gap meetings.
- Utilize checklists.

COMMUNICATION

Effective communication is not just the lead USAF Thunderbird pilot calling out maneuvers over the radio, or a Ranger fire team leader issuing orders to his riflemen. It's an overarching culture. It's a tactical plan. It's a strong web of interpersonal relationships. It's being able to convey a common message via a common language through each level of the organization so everyone is aligned.

Communication begins by reinforcing organizational identity and principles. This is where alignment begins. Good leaders constantly reinforce the bedrock principles of their unit, those things that define them, those things we always do or never do. When a team is working toward mission objectives, good communication will help each member understand how the current activities support the strategic plan for the larger group: *How will achieving this goal move us toward our HDD?* A step-by-step statement of how each level of planning relates to another creates line-of-sight alignment. When teams brief before moving to an execution phase, that alignment should be crystal clear.

Good planning is vital, whether your team is planning, communicating, or executing, and communication plans are as essential as any other. Good communication plans should incorporate that shared language that your team uses so there won't be any misunderstandings. The finished plan should clearly identify:

- The person who communicates and the channel he or she uses
- The person or people to be informed
- The message conveyed
- The date, or dates, of communication
- The intended effect or outcome

The military keeps it simple, and when important orders are involved, we will repeat them back and reconfirm. Many times, there is no margin for miscommunication, like when maneuvering a 100,000-ton, 1,100-foot aircraft carrier that is ultimately steered by a 19-year-old helmsman. As usual, the military has developed a process to simplify a complex operation.

The captain of a carrier designates an officer of the deck as the principle operator of the ship, responsible for setting the ship's course and carrying out its daily activities. He and the conning officer confer on speed and heading, and the conning officer owns responsibility for issuing the orders to the helmsman and lee helmsman. The helmsman steers the rudder, while the lee helmsman dictates the speed of the four screws that push the ship through the water. Orders related to speed and course are always repeated back and reconfirmed.

The conning officer will say, "Come right, steady on new course 290 degrees."

The helmsman will respond, "Aye sir, rudder is right, coming to course 290 degrees."

The conning officer reconfirms by saying, "Very well." If the helmsman does not hear "very well," he must repeat himself until the conning officer acknowledges with "very well." No margin for mistake.

It may seem trite, but when situations call for precise and confirmed communication, verifying information by repeating it back verbally or electronically can ensure your team remains aligned and executes according to plan.

One of the most elite military teams ever assembled relied extensively, and often entirely, on nonverbal communication. Through an ingenious communication network, this unit established a uniquely strong identity and became exceptionally effective at subverting its enemy through unified resistance.

During the Vietnam War, several hundred downed American pilots were held as prisoners of war in North Vietnam, many in the colonial garrison known as the Hanoi Hilton. From the moment the North Vietnamese captured their first American, they knew their success in bending the prisoners depended on their ability to isolate them and prevent them from communicating. Conversely, the American prisoners of war (POWs) instantly knew that maintaining communication with one another was vital to their unity, their ability to resist the communist propaganda and torture programs, and their very survival.

Under the leadership of fellow prisoners Bob Shumaker and Carlyle "Smitty" Harris, a group of early POWs adopted a secret code that would become the standard for the hundreds of POWs who would join them during the coming years. During his air force survival training, Harris had overheard a former Korean War POW discussing a tap code Americans had used to maintain communication while prisoners in North Korea. Harris and Shumaker thought the system fit their situation in Hanoi perfectly. POWs in adjacent cells had learned they could tap to one another through their walls; they just needed a code that their captors couldn't translate.

These clever POWs removed the letter K from the alphabet and placed the remaining 25 letters into a 5-by-5 matrix; C would substitute for K (see the table). The first row contained letters A, B, C, D, and E. The left-hand column contained A, F, L, Q, and V. To send a letter, a POW would tap the row, then the column. For example, Shumaker would send a C by tapping one time to indicate the row, then three times for the column. The POWs became prolific and highly adept at sending and receiving messages; they had nothing but time. One POW described the Hanoi Hilton as sounding like a den of woodpeckers. To speed the process, they abbreviated words just like their grandchildren would one day abbreviate text messages. Their typical signoff became GBU, which stood for God Bless You.

	1	2	3	4	5
1	A	B	C/K	D	E
2	F	G	H	I	J
3	L	M	N	O	P
4	Q	R	S	T	U
5	V	W	X	Y	Z

Leaders like air force ace Robbie Risner and navy commanders Jim Stockdale and Jeremiah Denton used the tap code, hidden notes, and the pervasive communication network to spread strict orders through the POW population. The men were not to bow to any North Vietnamese soldier in public, read any propaganda on the radio, confess to any crimes, or curry favor with their captors. They were to complain constantly about their conditions and remind the North Vietnamese that their treatment of the American POWs was in gross violation of the Geneva Convention. Above all, the POWs were to place unity above self. Through communication, the U.S. leaders established a powerful organizational identity, clarified their organizational imperatives, and kept up the POWs' fighting spirit.

One morning in 1967, the North Vietnamese Camp Authority announced an opportunity for POWs to earn special privileges by helping repair bomb damage in town. Their offer tempted many long-suffering POWs, but by that afternoon, when the North Vietnamese began asking POWs if they would accept, Stockdale and Denton had sent messages throughout the POW population forbidding any Americans from participating in what they knew was a propaganda stunt. The POWs held firm and remained unified because they knew their brother POWs were standing with them.

Through their communication, these men reminded each other they were Americans at war, not prisoners. They never lost sight of their identity or their mission. They endeavored to resist their captors and return home with honor. By maintaining their communication network and encouraging one another in resisting the North Vietnamese, they came home in 1973, after up to eight years of captivity, with their honor intact. Without effective communication, they would have had a very different story to tell.

Effective team communication:

- Reinforces organizational identity.
- Reinforces the big picture and creates line-of-sight alignment.
- Relies on briefing.
- Establishes a communication plan with clear responsibilities and timelines.
- Utilizes a common language.
- Repeats it back for comprehension.

KNOWLEDGE

The more complex our operating environment, the more important knowledge becomes to mission success. Today, we have access to more data than at any point in history. Satellites or unmanned aerial vehicles (UAVs) can provide battlefield commanders with real-time images of targets or terrain one mile or one hundred miles away. Intelligence can intercept messages and relay information to the field. Teams can share information instantly via phones and computers. The U.S. military enters battle with more knowledge at their disposal than any fighting force in history.

But no general, no lieutenant, no sergeant will ever have complete knowledge. An element of the unknown always remains in any plan or situation. When U.S. special forces left on the mission to capture or kill Osama bin Laden, they were still unsure of what or precisely who they would find in the Abbottabad compound, but they had a good hunch. The military and the CIA had gathered the best intelligence available, made the best plan possible, and trained relentlessly. So the president made the call: "Go." If the decision-makers had waited to know with 100 percent certainty that the tall man in the compound was bin Laden, the infamous al-Qaeda leader would still be at large.

Elite teams avoid analysis paralysis. They have the courage to act, even when they have less information than they'd like. They've trained and prepared for contingencies so well that they can improvise and adapt to almost any surprise. They may have a knowledge gap, but they'll make sure they don't have an execution gap. For them, *enough* information isn't necessarily *all* the information.

If knowledge isn't perfect (and it rarely is), the next best thing is assembling a diverse team, comprised of individuals with different perspectives and skills sets. Scholar Scott Page notes that "diversity trumps ability." Unfortunately, too many teams in American business are comprised of individuals with similar backgrounds or viewpoints. Successful execution in complex environments takes high-performance teams with a broad knowledge base who can see every aspect of a complex landscape. Diverse teams naturally close knowledge gaps.

So do lessons learned. Organizations like the U.S. Marine Corps, with its MCCLL database, increase their knowledge and close gaps by incorporating lessons learned in their planning and execution processes. Even the most diverse team won't have all the experience or all the perspective available, so the lessons learned by others offer the best way to close gaps and improve the quality of planning and execution. The challenge becomes capturing and organizing lessons learned in a way your employees and team members can access and use them. You must establish a process for effective debriefing and root-cause analysis, then capture the root causes electronically and tag or file them so they can be searched easily. For all of this to affect operations, a company must ensure teams *use* the data. Incorporating lessons learned must become an established and expected part of your planning process.

Effective teams:

- Take action and avoid analysis paralysis (knowledge is never perfect).
- Utilize cognitive diversity.
- Include subject-matter expertise.
- Capture, catalog, and incorporate lessons learned.
- Train to close knowledge gaps.

EXPERIENCE

Few things have never been done before, so don't shy from asking for help from someone who has been there before. If Green Berets are planning an assault on a hostile outpost in Central America, you can bet that they'll have experienced operatives involved in the planning process, either as team members or as part of the red team. They want someone involved who has been there before, literally and figuratively. They need that perspective to help identify situations they might realistically confront on the ground in a certain area, when dealing with a certain adversary, or using certain equipment.

This seems like common sense, of course, but I've seen youthful over-exuberance or over-confidence lead business teams to ignore or even shun experience to their own detriment. Yes, times, technologies, and methodologies do change, but that doesn't render experience irrelevant. There's a reason military teams almost always include higher-ranking members who have battlefield experience. You should make sure that same fire-tempered perspective is available for your teams, as well.

Regardless of who is on your team, you can accelerate your experience-building with effective debriefs. The best way to compensate for not having been in combat is learning as quickly as possible from your own experience. It goes back to debriefing. Effective debriefing is critical to improving your ability to execute and close execution gaps in the future. Do not underestimate the value of the nameless, rankless debrief and the STEALTH process.

Combat experience is expensive in more ways than one. So the navy developed a school that injects experience into fleet squadrons. It's their answer to the air force Weapons Instructor Course. In the film *Top Gun*, Mike "Viper" Metcalf tells students arriving at Naval Fighter Weapons School, "Gentlemen, you are the top one percent of all naval aviators. The elite. The best of the best. We'll make you better."[1]

More than 25 years later, that's still the goal of the navy's elite training program, now housed at Naval Air Station Fallon, Nevada. Today,

---

[1] *Top Gun*, directed by Tony Scott, 1986.

it's called the Naval Strike and Air Warfare Center (NSAWC). It combines training for navy fighters, helicopters, and E-2 Hawkeyes with training programs for entire carrier air wings. Over the deserts west of Reno, the navy's best get a little better through experience.

The terrain begins preparing aviators for their most likely battlefields: the barren lands and mountains of the Middle East and Afghanistan. The program has changed along with the nature of twenty-first-century battle. While fighters still train in air-to-air combat, they now conduct extensive training with other aircraft and ground-based teams like navy SEALs who are being trained at Fallon's Joint Terminal Attack Controller (JTAC) school. Working together, teams in the air and on the ground simulate likely scenarios: mountain strikes, rescue missions, and attacks on convoys. They call in artillery and other assets as needed, and ground-based assets and air-based assets gain experience working together. These exercises build critical skills in a safe environment, so while a pilot may have never flown over Afghanistan in combat, he or she has experience that's the next best thing. Combat is not the place to learn on the fly.

Since a carrier air wing operates as a team of teams, the training delivered at Fallon and NSAWC ensures participants leave knowing how to work together. The air wing program is called STRIKE. Entire air wings spend five weeks at Fallon. Aviators, NFOs, maintainers, and other personnel all take a mini-deployment where they'll work and train together each day, building combat-like experience in a carefully designed and controlled environment. In 10,000 square miles of Nevada airspace above and around Fallon, F/A-18 Hornets and Super Hornets, F/A-18G Growler electronic attack aircraft, H-60 Seahawk helicopters, and E-2C Hawkeye radar platforms fly missions together, just as if they were on their carrier.

"NSAWC tries to build air-wing integration," explained instructor Lee Amerine. "We teach them to function together. We're fine-tuning their skills so when they leave, they're at the top of their game and ready for deployment. They've already done a cycle of technical training and when they get to us, they learn game-time execution. It's no longer tactics in a vacuum. Air Wing Fallon puts you in the real world." It's about giving teams as much experience as possible in five weeks.

Naval Fighter Weapons School (TOPGUN) has become the Strike Fighter Tactic Instructor program, and like its air force counterpart, it aims to instill experience in carrier air wings by sending its graduates back to the fleet with a mission to train others, to disperse their experience into squadrons. For the duration of their next deployment, graduates are known as strike fighter tactics instructors. For the rest of their careers, they'll wear the SFTI patch on their shoulder. Their job is to accelerate the performance of their peers in the fleet.

By educating a cadre of instructors and by training entire air wings in concert, the navy ensures its teams have the experience necessary to perform in battle. Smart training by any organization prepares its team for the real thing; it gives them the confidence to perform under pressure.

Before the commercial cargo ship *Maersk Alabama* sailed into the Indian Ocean in April 2009, its civilian crew had received antipiracy training from the Seafarers International Union. They trained in small arms and other anti-terror tactics. In fact, they had drilled for a pirate raid the day before the actual attack occurred. When Somali pirates attacked, the crew was prepared; training had given them the experience they needed. They held the pirates at bay for several hours by using maneuvers and other tactics to make boarding difficult. Once pirates boarded and took the captain hostage, second officer Shane Murphy took over the ship and led the resistance. Murphy had graduated from the Massachusetts Maritime Academy where his father taught courses in repelling pirates. He knew to take charge and knew how to respond. The crew had no guns, but managed to disable the ship, capture one pirate, and hide for 12 hours. All of those steps bought time for the U.S. Navy to arrive on scene and track the pirates who were fleeing in the ship's lifeboat with the hostage captain.

Seven months after the April attack, Somali pirates attacked the *Alabama* yet again. The experienced crew successfully repelled the second attack using automatic and sonic weapons and a security team onboard the ship. Maersk and the ship's crew had learned from the past and worked together not to repeat it. Experience and preparation are essential to good execution.

Experienced teams:

- Red-team plans.
- Debrief to accelerate experience.
- Include experience on teams.
- Incorporate lessons learned.

DISCIPLINE

The navy has its Blue Angels and the air force has its Thunderbirds, but the army has the 3rd Infantry Regiment, the Old Guard, which includes the elite young men who guard the Tomb of the Unknown Soldier at Arlington National Cemetery. Every minute of every day, at least one of these men is keeping vigil in front of the tomb, marching in precise, respectful cadence. These sentinels keep their vigil throughout the coldest of winter nights and the hottest of summer days. In rain or snow, with spectators or alone, they never ease up. Every hour or half hour, in one of America's most exacting and famous displays of military ceremony, the guard changes.

Tomb guards are chosen through a rigorous process. Their knowledge of military and American history must be extensive and their service records exemplary. They must know, verbatim, countless pages of Arlington Cemetery history. The elite soldiers who are selected join a brotherhood that supports one another in one of the most disciplined posts in the armed forces. They all devote themselves to excellence and they draw the best out of each other. Prior to a soldier's leaving the guard chambers below the tomb for his shift, another guard will carefully inspect his uniform before two large mirrors, making sure not a single piece of lint or misaligned button mars the perfection of his ensemble. In front of the tomb, the sentry on duty marches with his back ramrod straight, his steps precisely measured, one polished boot placed directly in front of the other. Neither his pace nor his expression ever changes. At the changing of the guard, a sergeant performs a uniform and rifle inspection that is meticulously choreographed but very real. To the public's eye, their routines are perfect. Their discipline is so extraordinary because they consider it their tribute to the men and women buried at Arlington. Their discipline is also extraordinary because of their deeply ingrained organizational identity. Through their discipline, they pay respect; that's the Old Guard's singular mission.

The men of this special unit aim to honor our deceased servicemen and women; they have no higher priority. Devotion to the unit is their second focus, and self-service comes last. Like other high-performing military teams, they prioritize and focus on the most important results. In the case of the tomb guards specifically, their number-one task is to honor fallen unknown soldiers with a perfect, disciplined vigil. Because they have such laser focus, they can avoid the task saturation that affects many military teams. They learn to shut out all distractions as they stand their watch. To make sure their routine stays on track, they can make adjustments to their pace or timing each time they execute an about-face, and you better believe any mistakes are uncovered and fixed in a debrief.

Discipline relates to the team's ability to carry out the plan as it was designed, follow the execution rhythm, adapt by using X-gap meetings, and resist distractions. Almost nothing will distract a tomb guard from his duty; your team should maintain that same laser focus on its mission objectives. During execution, any team will have distractions: other projects, changes in the environment, or countless personal preoccupations. To execute effectively however, team members must compartmentalize those other issues to concentrate on the most important tasks related to their mission. Simply put, it's doing what you and your team are supposed to do. That's discipline, and it can become a hallmark of your team.

Stepping beyond the personal application, discipline can be a pervasive culture or mindset, like it is for the 3rd Regiment at Arlington. In high-risk occupations like aviation, oil exploration, or construction, strict adherence to polices and safety practices makes all the difference. Lack of discipline can cost lives or even millions of dollars in mistakes or legal penalties. In high-reliability organizations that function in arenas with little margin for error, discipline drives how team members act, communicate, resolve issues, maintain equipment, foster ownership, and manage the team. Having a strict and universal process enables organizations to operate safely and profitably.

Disciplined teams concern themselves with the mission objective, not the chaotic activity that may arise around achieving it. People often feel more comfortable when they're busy, but being busy is not necessarily being disciplined. Focus on the course of action instead of activities that might make you appear busy but that do little to move you toward the goal that matters most.

Self-generated busy work coupled with the actual work on a project can contribute to task saturation, so good teams always watch out for overloading and its symptoms: quitting, compartmentalizing, or channeling, which we covered in Chapter 5. At times, everyone feels they have too much to do and too little time. So when task saturation creeps into a team, just remember the antidotes: good planning, checklists, cross-checks, and task shedding. It's all part of good discipline.

Disciplined teams:

- Prioritize: objective, team, self.
- Focus on the objective: Results are more important than activity.
- Identify task saturation.
- Develop cross-checks.
- Use checklists.
- Have task-shedding plans.

CHAPTER 8

THE COURAGE TO EXECUTE: A SMART BIAS TOWARD THE RIGHT ACTION

If you have any doubt that business is combat, look at two companies who've shared the military story with countless Americans: Blockbuster and Netflix. In 2000, Blockbuster boasted 3,000 stores across the country and raked in revenue of roughly $5 billion. It was a goliath, the bane of local video stores. Five years later, it was struggling. At the end of the decade it filed for bankruptcy, then sold for a paltry $228 million.

Perhaps one of the early signs of Blockbuster's future came when they declined to buy a two-year-old DVD-by-mail company for the price of $50 million—a price that a company as large and profitable as Blockbuster could have easily afforded.[1] Five years later, that start-up company, Netflix, mailed out 1 million DVDs every day, was publicly traded, and raked in more than $500 million.[2] And it was eating Blockbuster's lunch.

Time waits for no man and consumers wait for no company. Heavily vested in its in-store business model and with millions in real estate on the books, Blockbuster tried holding on to consumer desires of the past. One business writer used a military analogy, comparing Blockbuster's faith in its retail stores to 1940 France's faith in the Maginot Line. Some inside the company had a hunch the market was changing, but they didn't act. Nexflix did, and because of their bias for action, they outflanked Blockbuster's store-based strategy just like the German army attacked France around the outdated Maginot Line.[3]

Netflix dispensed with the late fees that so riled consumers—and that lined Blockbuster's pockets to the tune of nearly $500 million per year. Netflix delivered DVDs to customers' doorsteps along with a return envelope, saving them a trip to the store. Instead of charging per rental, Netflix charged customers a flat fee. They moved quickly to address customer desires and by the time Blockbuster regained

[1] Megan O'Neill, "How Netflix Bankrupted and Destroyed Blockbuster," *Business Insider*, March 1, 2011. www.businessinsider.com/how-netflix-bankrupted-and-destroyed-blockbuster-infographic-2011-3.
[2] James Surowiecki, "The Next Level," *The New Yorker*, October 18, 2010. www.newyorker.com/talk/financial/2010/10/18/101018ta_talk_surowiecki.
[3] Ibid.

situational awareness and reacted, it was too late. The fight often goes to the aware and the swift, and the company that should have dominated the DVD-by-mail market (and later, the streaming market) flat-out lost to faster-moving competitors. Blockbuster could have offered physical presence, mail service, and online streaming. They had the capital to own the marketplace. But they were too vested in their current model to acknowledge the change and act. They lost situational awareness. They failed to incorporate new realities in their strategy. Competitors like Netflix saw the weakness and had the audacity to challenge Blockbuster because they knew they could be more nimble. They had a bias to action and the courage to execute.[4]

Just because you won a battle doesn't mean your enemy will disappear, however. Blockbuster emerged from bankruptcy and was acquired by DISH Network. It has once again joined the battle for online video and DVD marketshare and has moved to take advantage of slips made by Netflix and others. And Netflix, always adapting to the market, has moved from being a simple DVD provider to providing boundless online media content to actually producing content and creating its own shows. Management learned from the mistakes of Blockbuster. Netflix has rapid change and adaptation built into its DNA.[5]

It's like being a fighter pilot.

A bias toward action. We've seen it on battlefields and we've seen it on Wall Street and Main Street. The side that has it usually wins. Often, we're comfortable where we are. We think the turbulence of battle or the marketplace might pass us by if we just hang in there. That's like staying in a beach house because it's sunny outside at the moment, and naïvely hoping that the hurricane hurtling toward you will change course. Conditions change; realities change. But by using

---

[4]Ibid.

[5]www.newyorker.com/talk/financial/2010/10/18/101018ta_talk_surowiecki; www .businessinsider.com/how-netflix-bankrupted-and-destroyed-blockbuster-infogra phic-2011-3; www.insidetucsonbusiness.com/news/on_guard/a-case-study-in-lis tening-and-learning-from-mistakes/article_0bcc14ee-b356-11e2-b56f-0019bb296 3f4.html; www.businessinsider.com/how-netflix-bankrupted-and-destroyed-block buster-infographic-2011-3

the Flawless Execution cycle and these military principles, you can move at or above the rate of change. You can meet change head-on and turn it to your advantage. You can get inside your competition's execution cycle by reacting faster and more efficiently—like quarterback Peyton Manning trying to get inside brother Eli's cycle by debriefing after each series of downs. Companies can react and seize advantage by understanding the market conditions and having a process for continuous improvement that adjusts in real time.

Having a bias toward action requires the process and preparation we've discussed. It also requires some guts. You may not have all the information. You may run the risk of an embarrassing failure. Countless variables could affect your team and its mission. But when you know your battlespace is changing, you can't wait. You take the information you have, trust your processes and people, and go. Let's go back to the raid that killed Osama bin Laden.

In June 2009, President Barack Obama instructed Director of Central Intelligence Leon Panetta to develop a detailed plan for finding and capturing Osama bin Laden. The CIA had nothing to report for more than a year. Then in August 2010, Panetta reported agents had identified bin Laden's personal courier and had learned he lived in a compound in Abbottabad, Pakistan. The agency had identified another man in the compound, a tall figure who never left. Could it be bin Laden? Nobody had enough information to act yet.

In March 2011, the president reviewed tactical options for a raid on the compound. One option called for a helicopter strike, and Defense Secretary Robert Gates reminded the president of the ill-fated 1980 helicopter mission commissioned by President Carter to rescue American hostages in Iran. Eight Americans died and the special-operations mission never even made it to Tehran. The mission's failure still haunted the former president and the special operations community. The data available in 2011, however, suggested a helicopter strike by special operators would be best, and real training commenced, but it wasn't the troops' readiness or tactics that most worried the president. He didn't know if the mysterious man in the compound was, in fact, Osama bin Laden.

On Tuesday, April 26, 2011, the SEAL team that would ultimately kill Osama bin Laden flew across the Atlantic, en route to Afghanistan. The same day, Panetta reviewed the intelligence provided by the military and the Central Intelligence Agency (CIA). His experts placed their certainty that bin Laden was inside the Abbottabad compound between 40 and 99 percent. "This was a circumstantial case," they explained.[6]

Panetta called in experts from the National Counterterrorism Center to red-team the analysis. Their confidence in his intelligence reports rated between 40 and 60 percent. The center's director recommended waiting for more intelligence. Nobody was giving the secretary or the president the confidence they wanted. Here's what they did know:

- This was potentially as close as they'd been to finding bin Laden since he escaped Tora Bora in 2001.
- Tremendous resources had been invested in intelligence gathering and preparation for this mission.
- The figure in the compound fit bin Laden's description and actions inside the compound, like burning trash and having no Internet access, suggested something abnormal.
- They were entering a window of moonless nights over Abbottabad; perfect conditions for a raid.
- The SEALs were trained and ready, confident they could execute.
- A failure would rest heavily and publicly on the president's shoulders.

President Obama ended the meeting undecided. The next morning, however, he issued the order to go. He showed a bias to action. It was worse, he thought, to do nothing, letting the opportunity slip by, risking an intelligence leak, or letting the man inside the compound disappear. Neither the plan nor the intelligence was perfect.

---

[6]Nicholas Schmidle, "Getting bin Laden: What Happened That Night in Abbottabad," *The New Yorker*, August 8, 2011. www.newyorker.com/reporting/2011/08/08/110808fa_fact_schmidle.

One thousand variables remained, but the president decided to act. He and everyone down the chain of command had the courage to execute.

In military or business combat, organizations that wait for perfect information are doomed. It's possible they'll win occasionally, but fearful, hesitant organizations won't survive long in today's rapidly changing, complex environment. The pace of innovation and change is too fast. Survival demands action. Because there's no perfect information, we incorporate adjustment in our Flawless Execution engine. A company can move forward with an 80 percent plan and immediately start making headway in the marketplace, grabbing competitive advantage. By incorporating debriefing and a commitment to continuous improvement, the company can make incremental adjustments in strategy and tactics along the way. That 80 percent strategic plan becomes a 90 percent strategic plan and keeps improving from there—as long as you keep debriefing, planning, briefing, executing, and debriefing again in the tactical level. With every cycle, you should be incorporating lessons learned and be acting and adapting faster than your competition.

That's what gave President Obama the confidence to issue the order to launch the Abbottabad strike. That's what gave the SEALs the confidence to step out of the helicopters and into the dark uncertain compound in Pakistan.

That's the courage I'm talking about. That's the courage to execute. Everyone knew they were backed by a common process that works. Flawless Execution principles work for our military's elite teams and they work for businesses, NFL teams, PGA golfers, and any other organization you can imagine.

If you adopt these principles and follow the Flawless Execution model, you'll be one of those leaders who overcomes the persistent execution problem that plagues businesses around the globe. You'll have the courage and ability to execute because you'll have created an achievable high-definition destination (HDD) and, since you developed it with people from throughout your organization, team members will support it.

Business units and departments will have created well-defined high-definition destinations and associated metrics so everyone in the organization can measure their actions toward the universally-envisioned HDD. Will their actions help the organization achieve its goals and its HDD? If not, they should focus on other tracks.

A six-step planning process at the organizational, strategic, and tactical level generates plans that are backed by consensus, confidence, and situational awareness.

Teams will brief the plan before they act so everyone understands their individual role. Each person knows they're accountable, and when they execute plans, teams know to combat task saturation with task shedding and mutual support, crosschecks, and checklists. They hold X-gap meetings to close execution gaps rhythmically along the way instead of when gaps become too wide to cross.

At the end of the mission, the team holds a nameless, rankless debrief that identifies lessons learned and feeds them back into the planning process so the organization can continually stay one step ahead of the rate of change in their battlespace or marketplace.

America's elite military teams have proven that they have the courage to execute. We've done our best to help you understand the principles that have led them to success on battlefields around the world. In a way, our job was simple because the model that drives military success is also simple. These high-performing teams know that simplicity combats complexity. You don't need complicated models or expensive consultants to improve your execution level. Dan McAtee, a former General Electric executive who has led multinational steel and chemical companies, has implemented the simple plan-brief-execute-debrief cycle in several of his companies. "It's the best process out there," he said. "And that's coming from a Six Sigma black belt. Simplicity does combat complexity."

If your teams are so overwhelmed or hampered by procedures, complex data, and academic models that their execution suffers, there is a better way—a simpler way. If nimble competitors and a fast-changing marketplace are threatening your organization, there's a way to keep pace. All you need is a commitment to the principles and process behind Flawless Execution. Believe in them, adopt them, and you can survive, thrive, and dominate because your team will have the confidence, the process, the preparation, and the courage to execute.

APPENDIX

Mission Checklists

PLANNING OVERVIEW

Planning Questions

1. Is there another team in the organization working on a similar plan?
2. How much time can we dedicate to the planning process? Are we deliberate or rapid?
3. What is the purpose of this plan: action, contingency, or concept?
4. Do I have latitude in forming the team? Can I make it more collaborative and cognitively diverse?
5. Leader's decision brief: Is one required now or later for budget reasons or for clarity?
6. Budget check: The concept in planning that recognizes that budgetary approval during the planning process is required.
7. Communication plan: What level of communication will be required for team planning and for the organization?

Eighty Percent Planning

A good plan executed flawlessly is better than a perfect plan left on the shelf or implemented too late. You need a bias for action along with simplified plans that your troops can understand, support, and implement.

SIX STEPS TO MISSION PLANNING

1. **Determine the Mission Objective**
   a. Clear: Avoid proprietary or ambiguous terms unless the definition is agreed upon.
   b. Measurable: Provide a date when the mission objective will be measured, and ensure success or failure will be unambiguous at mission completion.
   c. Achievable: Does the planning team believe the mission objective is achievable?

    d. Aligned: Consider a description of how this mission objective supports the high-definition destination (HDD) and how it attacks critical leverage points in the strategy.

2. **Identify the Threats (to Accomplishing the Mission)**
    a. Internal: Controllable/uncontrollable
- Complacency, indifference, apathy to the mission
- Funding/resource priority
- Leadership support
- Expertise: internal subject matter experts
- Loss of critical personnel

    b. External: Controllable/uncontrollable
- Legal requirements and oversight
- Economic factors affecting your market or system
- Environmental crisis
- Uncontrollable threats in Step 6: Plan for Contingencies

3. **Identify Available and Necessary Resources**
    a. Subject matter experts
    b. People
    c. Products and services
    d. Vendors and partners
    e. Associations and trade groups
    f. Time
    g. Budget
    h. Other departments

4. **Evaluate Lessons Learned**
    a. Has anybody accomplished or been involved in a similar project/planning effort?
    b. Does anybody know anyone who has accomplished or been involved in a similar project/planning effort?
    c. Is there a knowledge system (lessons learned database) that we can access?
    d. Are there best practices or benchmarks available and applicable?
    e. Whom should we consult who has relevant information?
    f. Should we delay further planning subject to a lessons learned report?

Decision Point: Go/No-Go Decision

Evaluate the threats with regard to resources: Is there a compelling threat to the mission that does not have a resource that will negate or mitigate it? If so, consider briefing the leader on the situation.

Evaluate achievability: Is the goal achievable within time, resources (budget), and personnel allocated, and in light of the threats/resources review? If yes, keep planning. If no, brief leadership and consider extending the planning process.

5. **Develop a Course of Action**
   a. Divide the team into three groups of 3 to 10 planners.
      - Groups 1 and 2 build courses of action utilizing logical resources.
      - Group 3 builds a course of action using "unconstrained resource" thinking.
      - Each group presents their plan to the other groups.
      - The planning team integrates the three plans into one executable course of action.
   b. Red Team:
      - The course of action is briefed to a Red Team for review.
      - The Red Team voices concerns ("Have you considered …?").
      - The planning team considers Red Team concerns, and incorporates them in the course of action, ignores them, or addresses them in contingencies.
      - The course of action is finalized in a format that drives accountability (*who* does *what* by *when*).
   c. Final plan:
      - Formal debriefing is scheduled.
      - The course of action is briefed to leadership if approval is needed.

6. **Plan for Contingencies**
   a. Address uncontrollable threats.
   b. Consider "what if" scenarios and changes in:
      - Timing
      - Funding
      - Personnel

- Environment
- Administrative support

c. Establish a trigger/action matrix:
- Establish a trigger that unambiguously indicates the contingency is in effect.
- Establish the actions to be taken in response to the trigger.

BRIEF CHECKLIST

B: Brief the Scenario
- Roll call, set time parameters.
- Situation, big picture, tactical focus.

R: Review the Mission Objectives
- Comes directly from the plan.
- Clear, measurable, achievable, and aligned with HDD.

I: Identify the Threats and Resources
- Review the major obstacles to mission success.
- Review the major resources the team will use to negate or mitigate the threats to the mission.

E: Execution—Final Plan
- Confirm administrative procedures and standards and any deviations.
- Tactics and accountability: *who* does *what* by *when*.

F: Flexibility—Contingencies
- Identify the most likely contingencies.
- Brief trigger/action matrix.

EXECUTION CHECKLIST (TASK SATURATION REMEDIES)

Standards
- Administrative and tactical plans that are agreed-upon actions and reactions to specific situations.

Checklists
- Reduce the stress of forgetting your place or a routine step.

Cross-Checks and Task Shedding
- Maintain attitude indicator, and focus on the center of your cross-check.
- Work to shed tasks and share duties with others on your team.

Communication
- Clear, concise, and to the correct recipient.
- Company-critical information requirements.
- Clear guidance on what information must be immediately reported and to whom.

Clear Expectations
- Know the leader's intent.

Mutual Support
- Never leave your wingman, your most important resource.

STEALTH DEBRIEF CHECKLIST

S: Set the Time and Place
- The preparation phase—where and when?
- Who will participate?
- Define roles: leader, scribe, and others.
- What objective or milestones will be discussed?

T: Tone
- Nameless and rankless.
- Concentrate on events, not people (it's not *who* is right; it's *what* is right).
- Use "I," not "we."

E: Execution versus Objectives
- Restate the objective.
- Summarize actual results against desired results.
- Reconstruct the sequence of actions to assess success or error.

A: Analyze Execution
- Based on deconstruction.
- Results/event → cause (how) → root cause (why).

L: Lessons Learned
- Error/success.
- Course of action to implement.
- Single point of accountability.
- Time line.

T: Transfer Lessons Learned
- How will we share the experience?
- Accelerate learning.
- Techniques: notebooks, database, e-mail distribution, websites, blogs.

H: High Note
- Recap results, reinforce the positive outcomes, and have open dialogue on next steps.
- Reemphasize reason for pursuing the assigned objective.
- Show appreciation for each person's contribution.
- The leadership challenge: a strong, honest debrief that leaves your troops with their dignity.
- Stay on time; show respect for others' time.
- Schedule follow-up as needed, remember your rules of engagement, and use a "parking lot" to stay on track.

BIBLIOGRAPHY

Azinger, Paul. *Cracking the Code: The Winning Ryder Cup Strategy: Make It Work for You.* Kindle edition. Decatur, GA: Looking Glass Books, 2010.

Carabello, James, Command Sergeant Major, USA. Interview by author, August 8, 2013.

Carrion, Rick. Interview with the author, August 10, 2013.

Check Six, "The Crash of the X-31A," January 19, 1995. www.check-six.com/Crash_Sites/X-31_crash_site.htm.

Cink, Stewart. Interview by author, August 19, 2013.

Coldewey, Devin. "HP Attempts to Charge Customer $1,099 Due to 'Liquid Inside Keyboard,'" July 4, 2008. http://techcrunch.com/2008/07/04/hp-attempts-to-charge-customer-1099-due-to-liquid-inside-keyboard/.

Dao, James. "A Nation at War: The Commandos; Navy Seals Easily Seize 2 Oil Sites." *New York Times*, March 22, 2003. www.nytimes.com/2003/03/22/world/a-nation-at-war-the-commandos-navy-seals-easily-seize-2-oil-sites.html.

Demarest, James. Interview by author, August 17, 2013.

Ehrlich, Todd. Interview by author, August 1, 2013.

Freedman, David H. "Corps Values." *Inc.*, April 4, 1998. www.inc.com/magazine/19980401/906.html.

Haynes, Alex B., Thomas G. Weiser, William R. Berry, and Stuart R. Lipsitz. "A Surgical Safety Checklist to Reduce Morbidity and Mortality in a Global Population." *New England Journal of Medicine*, January 29, 2009. www.nejm.org/doi/full/10.1056/NEJMsa0810119.

Healy, Melissa. "Tactics Switch May Have Boosted Navy's Invasion Toll." *Lost Angeles Times*, January 27, 1990. http://articles.latimes.com/1990-01-27/news/mn-625_1_panama-invasion.

Hogerman, Chris. "Navy SEALs Hunting at Sea," April 7, 2013. http://navyseals.com/2186/navy-seals-hunting-at-sea/.

Horton, Ronald, Rear Admiral, USN (Ret.). Interview by author, August 2, 2013.

Hughes, Dana. "*Maersk Alabama* Battles Pirates for Second Time." *ABC News*, November 18, 2009. http://abcnews.go.com/Business/International/pirates-attack-us-flagged-maersk-alabama/story?id=9114429.

Kartvedt, Scott, Commander, USN (Ret.). Interview by author, July 25, 2013.

Kaufman, Ron. "Set the Stage for Continuous Improvement." *Chief Learning Officer*, August 8, 2011. http://clomedia.com/articles/view/set-the-stage-for-continuous-improvement.

Keeney, Douglas. *15 Minutes: General Curtis LeMay and the Countdown to Nuclear Annihilation*. New York: Macmillan, 2012.

Kowitt, Beth. "Inside the Secret World of Trader Joe's." *Fortune*, August 23, 2010. http://money.cnn.com/2010/08/20/news/companies/inside_trader_joes_full_version.fortune/index.htm.

Krulak, Charles, General, USMC. "The Strategic Corporal: Leadership in the Three Block War." *Marines*, January 1999. www.au.af.mil/au/awc/awcgate/usmc/strategic_corporal.htm.

Lowy, Joan, and Joshua Freed. "Delta Bag Fees for Soldiers Ignites Backlash." *Army Times*, June 6, 2011. www.armytimes.com/article/20110608/NEWS/106080304/Delta-bag-fees-soldiers-ignites-backlash.

Mallinger, Mark, and Gerry Rossy. "The Trader Joe's Experience: The Impact of Corporate Culture on Business Strategy." *Graziado Business Review* 10, no. 2 (August 2008). http://gbr.pepperdine.edu/2010/08/the-trader-joes-experience.

Marine Corps Center for Lessons Learned, August 2, 2013. http://mccll.usmc.mil/.

McAtee, Dan. Interview by author, August 19, 2013.

McCarthy, Gary. "The Marine Corps Lesson Learned System: An Assessment." Naval Postgraduate School, August 4, 2013. http://oai.dtic.mil/oai/oai?verb=getRecord&metadataPrefix=html&identifier=ADA283560.

McChrystal, Stanley. "From Forward Operating Base to Boardroom." *Wall Street Journal*, May 21, 2012, A15.

McGinnis, Mark. Interview by author, August 14, 2013.

McGreal, Chris. "Three Shots Brought Down Pirates Who Took *Maersk Alabama* Captain Hostage." *Guardian* [UK], April 13, 2009. www.theguardian.com/world/2009/apr/13/us-navy-maersk-alabama-bainbridge.

Mewbourne, Dee, Rear Admiral, USN. Interview by author, July 12, 2013.

Mott, Robert. Interview by author, July 10, 2013.

NASA. "Ice In or On Static System Cause of X-31 Crash." November 7, 1995. www.nasa.gov/centers/dryden/news/NewsReleases/1995/95-33_pf.html.

O'Neill, Megan. "How Netflix Bankrupted and Destroyed Blockbuster." *Business Insider*, March 1, 2011. www.businessinsider.com/how-netflix-bankrupted-and-destroyed-blockbuster-infographic-2011-3.

Pronovost, Peter, Dale Needham, Sean Berenholtz, and David Sinopoli. "An Intervention to Decrease Catheter-Related Bloodstream Infections in the ICU." *New England Journal of Medicine* 355, no. 6 (December 28, 2006).

Schmidle, Nicholas. "Getting bin Laden: What Happened That Night in Abbottabad." *The New Yorker*, August 8, 2011. www.newyorker.com/reporting/2011/08/08/110808fa_fact_schmidle.

Southwest Airlines. "2010 One Report: Employee Engagement and Recognition." www.southwestonereport.com/people_em_eng.php.

Spade, Marcus. "Army Approves Plan to Create School for Red Teaming." *U.S. Army Training and Doctrine Command, Office of Public Affairs*, July 13, 2005. www.tradoc.army.mil/pao/TNSarchives/July05/070205.htm.

Surowiecki, James. "The Next Level." *The New Yorker*, October 18, 2010. www.newyorker.com/talk/financial/2010/10/18/101018ta_talk_surowiecki.

Szalavitz, Maia. "Study: A Simple Surgery Checklist Saves Lives." *Time*, January 14, 2009. www.time.com/time/health/article/0,8599,1871759,00.html.

Trader Joe's. "About Us." (n.d.) www.traderjoes.com/about/index.

Weaver, Matthew. "Somali Pirates Pick on the Wrong Ship: *Maersk Alabama* Crew Included Graduate of US Anti-Piracy Academy." *Guardian* [UK], April 9, 2009. www.theguardian.com/world/2009/apr/09/somali-pirates-maersk-alabama-shane-murphy.

Williams, Brandon. Interview by author, August 19, 2013.

INDEX